FOR THE LOVE OF
STEAM

WESTON. 1986.

FOR THE LOVE OF
STEAM

DAVID WESTON

David & Charles

To the other love in my life, Mary

'A Britannia at Dent' (opposite title page)
oil painting, 30in × 20in
Iron Duke passes the signal box at one of my favourite spots

Contrasts at Bressingham, Britannia Pacific No 70013
'Oliver Cromwell' and Beckton Gas Works No 1 (Neilson & Co. Glasgow
1892) (endpaper, left*)*

'Victory' at Thursford, Mr George Cushing's magnificent Burrell Show-
man's locomotive (working pencil drawing) (endpaper, right)

A DAVID & CHARLES BOOK

Hardback edition published 1988
Paperback edition published 2002

Distributed in North America
by F&W Publications, Inc.

David Weston has asserted his right to
be identified as the author of this work
in accordance with the Copyright,
Designs and Patents Act, 1988.

ISBN 0 7153 9303 0 (hardback)
ISBN 0 7153 1375 4 (paperback)

Printed in China by Hong Kong
Graphics & Printing Ltd
for David & Charles
Brunel House   Newton Abbot   Devon

CONTENTS

ACKNOWLEDGEMENTS

My thanks are due to the following, who have kindly agreed to the inclusion of their paintings in this book:

Jim and Margaret Savage: *Blue Peter* at York'; 'A4 at Gleneagles'; 'Cogload Junction'; 'Castle at Work'; 'Northgates'. Mr John Petcher: 'Landscape at Dent'. Mr and Mrs Roy Watts: 'Derbyshire Yeomanry'; 'Ironstone Line'. Alan and Jean Jessop: 'Dark Day at Rugby'; 'Thurnby and Scraptoft Station'; 'Sizzling Steam'; 'Snow at Dent'; 'Down the Lotty'. Sir Peter and Lady Allen: *Mallard* at King's Cross'. David and Joan Mills: 'Smoke and Grime – Nottingham Victoria'. Graham and Wendy Smith: *The Master Cutler*'. Geoff and Joan Fillingham: 'Freight at Dent Station'; *Black 5* at Wild Boar Fell'. The National Railway Museum: *Witherslack Hall* on Shed'. Dr Leo and Debbie Ruth: 'Last Links with Tilton'. Jim and Diana Davies: 'Day's Work Done'; 'Harvester at Speed'; 'Britannia at Dent'. David and Carla John: 'A Ticket to Brooksby'. Mr Steve Herrick: 'The King Awaits a Reprieve'. The Hon. William McAlpine: '1941 and Britain at War'; 'A Carcass at Kettering'.

Mr Rex Blaker: 'A4 at York Station'; *Carlisle Citadel*'. The Jessop Collection: 'Mist and Dereliction'; 'No Place Like Home'; 'Requiem for Steam'; *Princess Alice*'; 'Rhondda Platform'; 'Wheels and Weeds'; 'Sunlight and Smoke'; 'Filtering Light, Pen Green Shed'; 'Sundown'; 'Sidelight'; 'Black and Gold Merthyr'; 'Dazzling Light, Groby'; 'Winter in the Barn, Bressingham'. Mr W. J. C. Ford: The paintings comprising the collection of 'Steam in Town and Country'.

My thanks are also due to Ken Adlard for his black and white photography of all the paintings that are not printed in colour, and to James Haworth Ltd for the loan of colour transparencies of all the traction-engine paintings.

I would like to thank also Sheila Cherry for her patience and expertise in typing my manuscript and my friend Christopher Wren for his invaluable help in collecting all the paintings together for reproduction, and lastly my wife who remains a steadfast pillar of strength despite the vagaries of her husband's artistic spirit and temperament.

FOREWORD

During 1978, an exhibition of my paintings depicting the story of the British steam locomotive arrived at Bressingham Steam Museum for a season's showing as part of its nationwide tour of Museums and Art galleries. Among the visitors to the private view was the distinguished writer and journalist Adrian Bell, who spoke to me at length about the pictures and of his own personal memories of steam as a boy in the early years of the century.

The following Saturday, 10 June 1978, *The Eastern Daily Press* published the following article entitled 'Best Way to Boil Kettles'. In it, the writer evoked the mystery and the wonder of the age of steam in words far finer than any I could write myself, so as a foreword to my own words and pictures, I would like to reprint Adrian Bell's thoughts after he had seen my paintings.

Best Way to Boil Kettles

Not for tea, but for steam. That was enshrined in the fable of James Watt and the kettle. 'While walking on a Sunday afternoon in Glasgow Green the idea flashed upon him that if the steam were condensed in a vessel . . .' That is how great things happen. Then Stephenson made steam pull a train. I never cease to wonder at beginnings.

I have just returned from looking at 24 oil paintings which amount to a pictorial saga of the years of steam, by David Weston. They are on display in Bressingham Steam Museum, flanked by the real presence of the Royal Scot, while *Oliver Cromwell* was getting up steam outside at that moment.

More than half the locomotives in these paintings were the latest developments in steam transport during some part of my own lifetime; types that had pulled me north, south, east or west to coast or country, starting at age two with my mother to Leeds and my nurse to Scotland. Then, age six, in 1907 came my first consciously enjoyed excursion from Paddington.

Each of these pictures is not simply a portrait of a locomotive, although the engine looks literal in every detail, but also a total composition, an evocation of a period. Faces of certain masters of the railway genius haunt those white wraiths of steam which engines breathe as they stand.

I found myself asking whence was born that genius to a man who herded cattle at an age when a boy of today would be sitting his O Levels, and was earning a shilling a day as assistant fireman at a pit when today a youth would be sitting his A Levels? I refer to George Stephenson, and at 18 he still could not read. Yet he produced this thing in the picture; look at it,

rather a barrel-shaped dream called the *Rocket* which got up a speed equal to the speed limit in a road in a built-up area today. And here also in the picture is his seal bearing George Stephenson's motto, 'Never Give Up'.

Only six years later than the *Rocket*'s feat Jane Carlyle dared the journey by rail from Manchester to Liverpool. She wrote home to her husband about it: 'A flight, it can be called nothing else, of thirty four miles in an hour and a quarter. I was dreadfully frightened before the train started . . . and the impossibility of getting the horrid thing stopped.' But after a few minutes she lost her fear of moving at 30 miles an hour. Progress was developing in the human mind also, to tolerate, even enjoy, 30 miles an hour.

Within 35 years of that occasion was evolved the most beautiful locomotive that ever was built, to my view, and I think David Weston's. It is No 5 of his portraits of steam. That could have been my father's first sight of a steam train, he being then of an age to be learning his ABC in Edinburgh, and the engine being Patrick Stirling's '8 ft. Single' on the Great Northern line of 1870. Look at it awhile: it inspires homage.

Locomotives of 1895 raced each other by different lines to Edinburgh and achieved almost an all-time record for the run. One of them must have carried my young mother-to-be on her visit to my father's parents as an engaged girl. The rate of development of rail speed is thus dramatically pictured: I was kept wondering at the collective genius which evolved so much so swiftly from the basic fact of boiling water. The actual great express engines of the culmination of the years of steam were here at my elbow in the museum to bear silent witness.

In a few years appeared engines of my own lifetime – even the train pictured waiting at Paddington in 1907. It was in that year that our family, small brother, baby sister, mother, nurse, and masses of luggage, entrained from Paddington departure platform for that first remembered holiday run into Oxfordshire. It whisked us through the changing landscapes of the counties. At Reading a man with a hammer came tapping the wheels, a regular bell-like sound.

Finally by a branch line we reached a steep grey village, where the whistle of a train from the cutting seemed just the call of some other bird of the mysterious country night.

By 1912 my schoolmates and I were obsessed by locomotives. We knew them all by the numbers of their driving wheels and bogies; a 4-4-0, a 4-4-2, a 2-8-0, 4-6-0 etc. They filled an area of our souls reserved for the heroic. From age 10 to 16 they were our gods. At 17 they began to be exchanged for poetry, romantic love, then adulthood and ordinariness. But some men, like my first publisher, remained steam enthusiasts to their dying day. At 12 I had a toy stationary engine that worked: shrieking safety valve, racing piston; fearsome microcosm of power.

Dynamism is the secret of all. At 17 my own dynamism shifted from steam to words. It happened in a moment. I was in class reading a set book. Two lines did it: 'The moan of doves in immemorial elms, and murmuring of innumerable bees.' Just that, and seeing a horse-drawn plough turning tough earth like a wave of water. Possibly David Weston could point to some such moment which attracted him to this exhalation of iron that lives in the wraiths of steam, powerfully compressed, then let float away in snowy clouds, thinning to lacy wisps impregnated with blue sky and vanishing in air. He has by heart the anatomy of locomotives, as Munnings had by heart the bones and sinews of a horse.

Not for the first time I asked myself, does not conventional schooling stuff too many facts into a child's head as history lengthens out and scientific discovery widens? Is the young idea left with any room to shoot, the native genius to awake and wonder? Myself, I refused to learn at school what I did not want to learn, as soon as I was awakened by that flash of verse to the dynamism of words. Others had been as imperatively called by the dynamism of fire and water, and the original artist by his vision of those iron horses as living creatures, breathing air into their bellies of fire and breathing it out in power.

Adrian Bell, Norfolk 1978

INTRODUCTION

This book is a celebration of the steam engine in all its forms. The paintings reflect the fascinating age of steam and all the paraphernalia that accompanied it as seen through the eyes of an artist who is an incurable romantic. I have a great love of the landscape and nature, a love of architecture, and a fascination with all forms of transport whether on sea, air or land, but in particular with the latter – a love of steam.

The paintings in this collection, therefore, will demonstrate a considerable variation within the scope of the subject matter and at the same time show how an artist can, on the one hand, revel in the expression of mechanical detail while, on the other, having a regard and understanding for the broad atmospheric effects of light, steam and smoke that were so redolent of the age of steam.

As a boy growing up in the Forties, I saw a great deal of post-war steam and have some strong memories of engines in their pre-1947 liveries before the big four companies became British Railways. At the same time, I became aware of an urge to draw and paint, so the two interests became, even at an early age, inextricably intertwined. At junior school, drawing steam engines that could be seen only a few hundred yards away on the Midland main line seemed natural and led to my first 'real' paintings that were done in 1949.

It is a striking thought that by the time this book is published and in the hands of the reader, my brushes will have been painting pictures for about forty years; exactly half of that time was spent as an enthusiastic amateur, while the last twenty years have afforded me the privileged life-style of a professional painter. I say privileged because to secure a livelihood from an activity that one would pursue if one didn't need to earn a living at all is, coupled with the great freedom it affords, a great privilege indeed.

As my story will reveal, this privileged life-style was not achieved without some hardships and a tenacity to continue with my chosen path, believing that I would win through in the end. Although it took twenty years to achieve my goal of painting full-time, a certain sincerity has been maintained within my work from those early years of trial and error. Whatever goes into making a painter successful, an essential ingredient is to be totally honest with oneself and to paint from the heart in the way that the years of personal effort have evolved.

It takes time for a painter to find his style – his own handwriting as it were – one that is instantly recognisable from anyone else's. Every painter will be influenced by the work of others, of course, especially those whose work they may hold in high esteem, and it would be a dull world if all painters transmitted their thoughts onto canvas in the same way.

My own style or technique was slow to evolve and, like my career as a whole, took a devious route. I began working in a traditional, or representational style, first in watercolours and later in oils, striving to improve my ability to paint with clarity and sensitivity; so my style in oils altered over several years, from careful handling with the brush to a much broader method of brushwork, then to the application of oil paint with a knife, and then returning to an earlier style – it was experimentation in order to ascertain the way ahead.

In later years, my techniques became influenced by more modern styles and modern painters, with artists like John Piper and Ivon Hitchens whose semi-abstraction held sway with me in no uncertain terms. Hitchens' inspiration lay in landscape, woods, fields and vast valleys, while Piper's imagery stemmed mainly from architecture. I absorbed the styles of both artists, and their methods became reflected in my own pictures so that I pursued a semi-abstract style for a number of years.

Gradually, my work became so abstract that I no longer drew inspiration from nature, but after two or three years along this course I realised that abstraction was not the way ahead. Although not regretful of that period of work because I learnt a considerable amount about design, colour and textures, ultimately I returned to a more figurative style of work because I realised that I was going along a blind alley and that the vital expression of visual inspiration was being largely ignored in the process.

The return to a representational style came first through pop-art, a movement that influenced and fascinated me in the early Sixties, and then to surrealism in which some wild ideas were indulged, before the journey of experimentation was over.

All the journeys into the various forms of art-expression led to the general improvement of two aspects of my painting – conception and technique – so there were no regrets about the diversions; I accepted them as a foundation for future work and saw them as distinct advantages rather than time wasted. In the process, an appreciation for all forms of art was gained which lasts with me to this day.

My enquiring eye into other styles of artistic expression had taken some five or six years of my painting life at a time when I should have been observing

Myself as a young man in my attic studio (Leicester Mercury)

the changing railway scene; yet there seemed little point in going out to draw either landscape or railways when the motivation for picture-making lay either within my own mind or in the trigger of events past and present at the time. In my pop-art period, such events as World War I or the death of President Kennedy, and the Beatles' song 'Eleanor Rigby', were the inspiration for subjects; it was a far cry from depicting the dying years of the steam age, but thank goodness I returned to looking at the railways again before it was too late.

That slow drift back to observing steam engines as subjects for my brush proved to be fortuitous and led ultimately to the achievement of my long-held ambitions to paint full-time, but as the next three chapters will reveal, that achievement was not reached without either incident or hardship, and most certainly not without the fact that I had continued to paint railway pictures when all the advice was to the contrary.

So let me take you back to where it all began, to the day when the two aspects of my life that are the cause and subject of this book came together for the first time in the moment of encounter with a fiery dragon in full cry.

Northgates, Leicester
oil painting, 30in × 20in
One of the Great Central's girder bridges, typical of its route through
Leicester

1 AND ALL FOR THE FEAR OF THE FIERY DRAGON

There was nothing new about the sound, that sharp, barking roar that filled the clear air of a November evening. I had heard it many times before. Dusk was settling in, cold and bleak, with already a glimpse of a star high in a cloudless sky.

From my position on the railway bank, as always on my way home from school, I could see in the distance the huge plume of smoke shooting upwards to meet the stars, but then, as the great iron monster drew nearer, I sensed that something was wrong this time, something that filled me with a sense of foreboding, almost of panic. The noise filled my head as by now the beast was upon me, a great pounding monster that was a mass of flame and obvious peril.

As the engine rushed past, it gave me a close-up vision of the fire as it leapt from the fire-box out and over the coals in the tender-top, tingeing the plumes of black smoke to a brilliant orange glow and singeing the silhouetted image of a desperate fireman hanging out of the cab as he struggled to knock closed the fire-box doors. It was indeed, to my young and impressionable eyes, a dragon in full cry. It made me scramble down that railway bank never to dare venture so close again for many a long day to come.

Back home, my story was recounted of the train that was on fire and for the first time I took out a sheet of paper to paint a bright and lurid splurge of the vision that was still dramatically impressed upon my mind. Little did I know then, at the age of eight, that what was happening at that moment in time was a portent of things to come in adult life; that the impelled and inspired childish splurge of paint would be recalled almost half a century later as my first-ever railway painting.

I cannot help wondering what happened to that painting. It no doubt went the way of many hundreds of its successors over the first few years of my covering paper with paint – on the bonfire. Now, of course, the desire to have the picture as a symbol of the start of a whole career or simply as a souvenir of childhood is from time to time a thought that comes to mind.

So the fiery dragon has much to answer for, and it is an extraordinary fact that railways and my natural instinct to paint came together very early in my life. Even later, while I was employed in various unrewarding jobs, no connection between the railway and my passion for painting pictures was realised in terms of earning a living – the railway was simply an occasional subject for a painting.

A true talent to paint is inborn, although where mine came from is difficult to imagine. Neither my father, an engineer, nor my mother was artistic and if there was any family throwback at all, it came in the shape of my father's elder brother, Harold. 'Uncle' was a draper and during the years of my childhood following the war, he had a small business in the front room of the terraced house he shared with his diminutive wife Edna.

Harold was a good 6ft tall, lean and bespectacled, with clothes that were always ill-fitting and darned beyond belief – the epitome of the well-dressed draper. There were always guarded nudges that he had done quite well over the 'black market' during the war, but his denials were perhaps a little too vehement and, despite his appearance, time showed that he had indeed been a shrewd businessman.

What fascinated me as a young boy was Uncle Harold's remarkable ability to turn a piece of blank paper or card into a vision of beautiful countryside. To me it was sheer magic; only, I thought, could a magician perform such incredible acts and my uncle was held in the highest esteem. For hour after hour I would stand by his elbow as he sat at his table in the comfortable living-room behind the shop. Often his careful nature precluded the warmth of a good fire in the hearth, but the magic appeared nonetheless from hands covered in ragged mittens, a cigarette dithering perilously on the edge of his lower lip.

He rolled his own, flat, weedy cigarettes that constantly caused him to spit out tobacco onto his wet painting, but worse would follow when, due to the effort of controlling a wet wash on a large sky, he would forget the cigarette altogether until the long drooping tube of ash would suddenly deposit itself in the middle of his almost-completed sky. Needless to say, the language was as educational as the painting demonstration itself, and the resultant failure was furiously torn up. I witnessed such a charade many times over.

My uncle's careful nature also caused him to steer clear of good quality watercolour paper. His preference, unbelievably, was for the backs of box-lids from the shop. Ladies' stocking-boxes were best liked and often there was what might be considered to be a ludicrous discussion on the relative merits of silk or plated stocking-boxes as opposed to those containing lisle hose, and often his consumption of boxes outstripped the rate of sale for their contents, with the result that there were always piles of stockings with no boxes in the shop – a situation to which an irate aunt made her disapproval well and truly felt.

To a boy's eyes, the apparent ease with which my uncle turned an old box-lid into a recognisable local beauty spot was a tremendous feat and consequently I longed with every breath in my body to be able to do the same. Harold responded to this and soon we were going out sketching and painting together on Sunday mornings to capture the delights of Swithland woods or Bradgate Park on paper, – or box-lids!

It soon became apparent that the art of watercolour painting was not as easy as the practised hand made it appear. The washes so flowingly applied by my uncle's confident brush were like half-dry mud in my hands, and the freshness which is so much the essence of the medium disappeared every time in a morass of overpainted sludge, so deceptive is the ease of the simple watercolour. I did have a natural ability with perspective which was somehow second nature, and my uncle commented that his first attempt at a subject would be either too large or too small, whereas my efforts were usually the right proportions the first time around.

Sunday mornings were the highlight of my week, and as Allen's old blue bus groaned around the corner by the Talbot Inn, my head and heart were filled with a soaring anticipation and excitement at the prospect of the paintings that my uncle and myself might produce.

This, then, was my introduction to the world of picture-making. I had slipped into it through a back door in awe and wonder of the type of art that Harold himself called outdated and finicky and which in time I would discover that the art-world in general dismissed as 'chocolate-boxy' and of little account. In retrospect, this was not perhaps the best introduction to art, but at least under my uncle's influence, the raw beginner was learning fast both to appreciate nature and to observe how plants grew.

Harold's forte was painting trees and he taught me to study the growth of tree and plant form. He emphasised repeatedly how sunlight filters over and through a tree, the branches casting their own shadows across the trunk, and how that same tree reflected in water is not just an inverted image, but has a certain degree of foreshortening. In short, Harold taught me to 'see' – an essential lesson for any novice.

Our weekly painting trips were invariably spent among the fields and woods of the pleasant Leicestershire countryside. For me, however, there were other delights worth considering, such as the wharves and tow-paths of Leicester's canal. The gas-works and the power station were all exciting visually and a little further along, just beyond the generating plant at the side of the canal, there was the dark and forbidding form of the old Great Central engine-shed. I longed to paint in there, but Harold would not consider it: such a mucky old place was of no interest to him and he suggested that if I wanted to paint in such a barren spot I should bicycle there during the week.

My bicycle became my saviour and whenever it was possible, I pedalled off at every opportunity during my last few years at school in search of subjects to paint. I grew to know every inch of Leicester's canal system from one end of the city to the other, it was so full of interest.

Of particular interest to me was an ancient lift bridge which was regarded with both fascination and not a little foreboding. The bridge was, in fact, built

'Sunlight and Steam'. Holbeck shed, Leeds. Painted in 1974 from previous drawings, the scene epitomises for me the dramatic atmosphere of a great steam shed.

by Robert Stephenson to carry the railway line over the water at Soar Lane for access to the coal yards of Ellis and Everard on the western bank and was part of the system of the old Leicester to Swannington railway which was opened in July 1832. The line was an immediate success and in fact re-established the prosperity of the West Leicestershire coal-mining industry in the county.

The bridge itself was stark, black and dramatic, a huge gallows-like structure with great baulks of timber supporting the overhead pulley wheels and chains that in turn lifted the bridge platform with its section of rail a few feet higher to allow canal boats to pass underneath.

I always felt thankful on rounding the bend on the tow-path to see

(page 14) 'Reflections'
oil painting, 14in × 10in
A watery sun and harmonies of cool greys reflect in the waters of the Leicester Canal at Seven Bridges (Jessop Collection)

(page 15) The Master Cutler
oil painting, 30in × 20in
No 60107 'Royal Lancer' departs from Leicester for Marylebone

WESTON.

the bridge lifted, for it meant that I could pass underneath on foot almost upright. If the bridge was down, it meant that I would have to crouch down and scramble underneath, the height between the underside of the bridge and the tow-path being only about 3ft. To struggle through with a bicycle was always an experience I was glad to put behind me.

Naturally, I made numerous sketches of it despite the fact that the narrow cramped conditions of the canal at that point allowed little option as far as the viewpoint was concerned, but the bridge transmitted an ancient and dramatic image that my senses responded to in no uncertain way.

Further north, there were the remains of the once-busy wharf at Painter Street, overshadowed by huge gasometers and the acrid smells of the coking plant. The old buildings that were once the busy warehouses of Fellows, Morton & Clayton looked down in dilapidation onto the dank waters of deserted bays. It inspired me to paint a large oil in later years of the same wharf in its heyday, the scene alive with steam-driven narrow boats unloading their cargoes, the cranes and winches oiled and in action – which was all so different from the rusting hulks that were a part of my boyhood memory. Either way, the boats made painterly material, as did the yards and shed of the then LNER at a point called locally Seven Bridges.

In those years, more often than not my bicycle could be seen chained to the battered railings of the canalside at that spot, even when I was truanting from school. Invariably, I would creep around in terror of being discovered by the shed-master and because I was within such close proximity to the towering giants of the steam age as they simmered, hissed and gurgled their warnings to a young lad with a sketchbook in one hand and an Ian Allen loco-spotter's guide in the other.

The deep gloom at the canal end of the engine-shed was entered by a tiny open doorway in the middle of the vast end wall of the building. I always approached it with a thumping heart, but once inside, the rewards were great – Directors with names such as *Butler Henderson, Somme, Zeebrugge, Mons, Jutland* and *Prince Albert* stood in line. Two or three of them could always be seen alongside the three cylinder V2s and now and again a Sandringham 4-6-0 with its massive 6ft 8in driving wheels towering high above my head.

Of all of the locomotives on Leicester's LNER lines, to me the Directors were the best. Built originally for the Great Central Railway by J. G. Robinson, they were in service from 1913 and were perhaps one of the most handsome of the 4-4-0s ever built.

As seen in their original Great Central livery of deep green and indian red, they must have been splendid, as is suggested by the now preserved *Butler Henderson* in the national collection, but in the late Forties they were black, often grimy and in poor condition. As far as I was concerned, however, they were real working engines, they emitted smells of smoke, sulphur, hot oil and steam, and I thrilled at being so close as to feel the warmth from their fires as my hand nervously tried to sketch in an outline of their elusive shapes.

To capture in paint the overwhelming subtleties of the light within such an interior was futile; my abilities were no match for it, and unfortunately dozens of the drawings and paintings that I produced at that time were torn up as being of no value. Forty years later and with the experience of the intervening years, good use could be made of those amateurish scribbles.

The visual memory of all that was seen in my formative years as a young artist has not faded, however. My memories of the engine-shed, for instance, are as clear to me now as they were when I was a lad. Perhaps it was partly the accompanying fear of trespassing that impressed so vividly the sights and sounds of the place onto my mind, but no doubt it was also due in some measure to my early training to observe carefully all that I saw and drew which developed the photographic memory that comes to an artist with years of constant endeavour.

Recently, on finding one of my early sketches, I was inspired to paint again a picture of one of those old Directors simmering gently in the deepest gloom of that shed with an illuminating sunlight filtering through the smoke ducts and mingling with the smoke and steam from the locomotive. It was an exercise painted entirely from memory and experience and with the aid of only the merest amateurish scribble as a starting point.

Little of Leicester's industry was not marked down to record as I cycled around the city. I was totally enraptured by industrial subject matter and paid more attention to that than to where I was going. Disaster eventually struck in a most undignified and embarrassing way, and, to make matters worse, the greatest damage was suffered by my brand new Hercules bicycle.

I did, of course, notice the red waterworks flag on its iron rod sticking up from a small drain in the middle of the road – I cannot deny that. I was also aware of the lunch-time bus-drivers and conductors sitting on the pavement outside their depot enjoying their sandwiches and tea, but my own sights were rather more taken with the misty autumn sunlight as it shafted through a line of glorious trees with the blue silhouettes of distant factory chimneys drifting their smoke across a perfect afternoon sky.

Then, suddenly, there was a whirling kaleidoscopic vision of bus drivers, sunlit trees, sky, chimneys and hard cobbled road – I had somersaulted over the handlebars. For a second or two, I just sat on the cobbles, still facing the way in which my bicycle had been travelling, but now to the accompaniment of rousing cheers from an audience of hysterical busmen. On turning to see what had happened, there, to my chagrin, was my new bicycle wedged firmly onto the iron rod with its red flag flying triumphantly above the handlebars, the bicycle otherwise remaining perfectly upright.

(page 18) Smoke and Grime, Nottingham Victoria
oil painting, 24in × 20in
No 2663 'Prince Albert' is lit in the deep cutting entering the station

(page 19) 'Sunlight and Smoke'
oil painting, 16in × 12in
Filtering sunlight and a Director in the gloomy depths of Leicester Great Central shed

The Great Central at Northgates, Leicester (working drawing)

On another occasion on the canal-side, my attention was suddenly arrested by the view upstream as I was lifting my bicycle down some steep steps. The light on the water, and the composition of a distant church and group of buildings made me stop in my tracks; the front of my bicycle was suspended while I carefully considered the view as a subject to paint. Having absorbed the view, I continued lifting my bicycle down the steps and lowered the handlebars towards the ground, only to be astonished by the fact that the front forks went down much further than expected. They went down so far, in fact, that I fell over in the act of trying to keep my balance.

The front wheel had completely disappeared. Bewildered by this incident, I wondered if it was all a dream, but then a gentle splash and an ever-widening circle of ripples some twenty-five yards upstream revealed its ghastly tale: the wheel had obviously dropped straight out of the untightened front forks and bowled along the tow-path to its demise in the canal.

How I was going to explain that particular incident at home caused me great concern and embarrassment as I walked homewards, suspending the handlebars of only half a bicycle. I also began to realise that a desire to draw and paint mechanical objects did not necessarily mean that one had an accompanying ability to manage them – this notion has remained with me to this day.

My persistence, however, at practising the delicate art of watercolour painting outside led me in time to become less timid about setting up an easel in full view of the public. Usually, when people approached me to look at my pathetic efforts, they would either go away in an embarrassed silence or ask if I had always been like that, as if I was suffering from a terrible illness or deformity, or they would inform me that they had a brother or a cousin or an aunt who 'really could paint'.

By degrees, however, I gained more confidence and eventually the time came when my painting on the easel was a reasonable impression of the scene before me. It was in Leicester's New Walk, a tree-lined walk that ran close to the city centre, that I felt for the first time pleased with my efforts. The painting did, after all, reflect the soft autumn sunlight with a distant pearly silhouette of a church spire, and I felt that I would not be embarrassed if people came and looked at my efforts.

I continued working on the painting, adding the finishing touches and almost willing an audience to gather. Eventually, a rather bent old lady appeared with two heavy shopping-bags which she rested on the ground with a gasping sigh. She straightened up a little and looked intently at my painting, then she scrutinised the view it depicted and re-established her concentration on the picture, slowly nodding but still silent. Then she picked up her bags and started on her way again, hesitated, and came back a few steps. Then, from her bent position, she looked me straight in the eyes and said, 'Well, never mind, me dear, you're getting the fresh air, aren't you?'

Perhaps I should say no more for a while about the trials of learning to paint out of doors for fear of discouraging those who have aspirations in that direction, but suffice it to say that all those experiences helped to form a firm foundation for a future artistic career that in those early years certainly looked like a non-starter, despite the overwhelming weight of enthusiasm I felt for the task.

My enthusiasm to improve my technique gave me the courage to knock on the door of Stanley Read, commonly known to be an artist, to ask if we might sometimes go out painting together, and further, if he would help with constructive criticism of my work.

Stanley, a bachelor, took me under his wing and as a result I became a regular visitor to the house he shared with his mother and two sisters. Mrs Read was even more of a character than her son and she dominated the household as the great matriarch. Her appearance was gipsy-like, from her weather-beaten face and dangling earrings to the flourishing head-scarf that she wore indoors and out. 'Ah,' she would say, 'It's all in the cards, lad', whenever I expressed the great desire to be a successful full-time painter. 'If it's in the cards, lad, you'll be all right.' She was a great believer in 'the cards', but one couldn't help noticing that she never indicated what they actually did say.

Stanley's passion was for watercolour – not the sunny pretty scenes that Uncle Harold so much enjoyed, but atmospheric, dramatic subjects that portrayed the worst of the English weather and moreover objects that were in a state of dilapidation, decay and dereliction. Allotments were therefore a frequent hunting ground for our material and if the day was dreary, wet, misty or snow-covered, the better Stanley liked it.

'He gets the spherics, you see, lad,' his mother would often say. 'His pictures are full of it, all that wet, its the spherics, ain't it?' I would readily agree, Stanley certainly did appear to get a liberal dose of 'the spherics' in all his paintings; in fact, as he worked on paper previously soaked in a bath of water or, if we were outside, liberally doused with water from a large brush, much of what he so earnestly painted would run totally out of control in a steady progression down the sloping surface of the paper.

The choice of allotments as subject matter suited me also and more often than not I would steer him towards those that ran alongside the old Belgrave and Birstall station on the Leicester to Sheffield route of the LNER. Once there, I would gravitate towards the line and more than once painted a railway subject while my colleague was attempting yet another ramshackle old shed surrounded by oil-drums. He didn't exactly approve of my propensity to paint the railways; it was, he submitted yet again, rubbish, and that it seemed was that. Unfortunately, I had set off on the wrong foot with him over my railway pictures because the first one ever shown to him was a brightly coloured paint-ing of the recently out-shopped LMS Pacific *Queen Elizabeth* at Rugby Station. 'It's like a picture for a kid's train-set box,' he had said with an equal degree of vehemence and disgust. I should, of course, have shown him an atmospheric picture of a dirty engine in a rain-storm, then perhaps I might have stood a better chance of persuading him to take the subject matter seriously.

But the die was cast and Stanley's disapproval deepened as I continued to produce railway paintings; even those full of damp or dramatic atmosphere were waved away with an intolerant gesture of rejection. Somehow, he was convinced that pictures of railway engines were only for jigsaw puzzles and train sets. It was difficult for me either to understand or accept such a blinkered vision on the part of another artist, and inevitably our friendship gradually diminished.

Mrs Read endeavoured to sum it up when she said: 'You're not painting the spherics, lad, that's your trouble. Chuck them trains up and get back to what our Stanley likes to paint – you won't go wrong.' I attempted to explain that there was just as much atmosphere in many of my railway paintings as there was in Stanley's allotment huts or derelict houses, but it was futile to attempt to convince either of them. 'Ah, well, you see lad, it's them trains. You can't have spherics in the trains, can you?'

I gave up trying to convince them. It was the very first time in my young life as a painter that I had met with such outright prejudice against railway subject matter, but of course it was most certainly not to be the last as the future years were to reveal.

The influences, both good and bad, of other painters, are at the end of the day a matter for sorting out dispassionately, listening to all the advice offered, and then ultimately following one's own instincts. For me in those early days, there had been the two extremes of my uncle whose ideas and abilities led him to paint in an old-fashioned, pretty style, and Stanley Read whose dogmatic views allowed him to believe only in his interpretation of the atmospheric and the dramatic.

A wealth of progress and inspiration was to be found between these two extremes which in any case would incorporate much of what had been learnt from both of these painters. The experience left me with an open mind and I have tried to maintain that balance throughout my painting years. The way ahead seemed clear enough: to enjoy painting all subject matter – I loved landscape work and much enjoyed architecture, and preferred to paint atmospheric pictures rather than sunny ones, and above all still felt a great desire to paint railways, despite all the advice to the contrary.

That I should want to paint at all was something that many of the teachers at my science-orientated school seemed unable to understand. A student who was not aiming at entering politics, the sciences, the Church or the Law, was considered a failure. However, I decided to opt out of the science section for a period in the art room, although a permanent art teacher was seldom available and the tuition that was given was sparse to say the least. However, with a bundle of my watercolours under my arm, I stood before the headmaster and requested that I should train as an artist. To my surprise, he was outraged at the very idea. 'You gibbering little idiot,' he shouted, 'You can't do that; you're good with your science. Who wants to be a Rembrandt anyway? Where would the world be if we all wanted to be flaming Rembrandts?' I didn't know or care, and was too taken aback by the enraged figure standing before me to say anything. The headmaster flicked impatiently at the pile of pictures on his desk without looking properly at even one of them and impatiently thrust them back at me. 'You'll have to tell Mr Goddard yourself. I daren't tell him,

but if he says it's all right, I'll accept it. But you're wasting your time. It's ludicrous. Painting pictures will never get you anywhere.'

To have to tell Archie Goddard what my plans were was a terrifying thought; I had hoped to get away without actually doing that myself. At the next lesson, I was standing before him and, having stammered my desire to become an artist, I looked up into his huge red face. His waxed moustache bristled and his eyes bulged. 'Art? Art? Art? What the hell's art?' he exploded. I endeavoured to explain that science no longer held any future for me and that a life in the arts was all I desired.

The class, now sitting in a hushed silence, waited eagerly for the next move. The silence was broken by one of my supportive and brave, if foolhardy, young friends who chirped up, 'He's very good, sir, he only wants to be an artist.' 'Shut up, you little bugger,' Archie retorted vehemently. 'I'll decide what he's going to be. He's going to be thrashed, that's what he's going to be.' He reached for the gym slipper that was standard procedure for the task. 'Artists have to suffer, you know, Weston, did you know they had to suffer?' 'Yes, sir,' came my timid reply. 'Ah, well, you can start now, bend over that desk and we'll soon see who wants to be an artist.'

There was nothing for it but to submit, and with every swish of that painful slipper he chanted 'You'll – never – make – a – living – as – a – blasted – artist.' Ten swipes. I sighed with relief, he had not finished yet. 'What won't he do boys?' he asked, and together they chanted his words again except that they all said 'sir' at the end and with it he delivered an extra hard swipe.

Twenty-one painful swipes, and as I stood up to face him he said: 'Now, Weston, do you still want to be an artist?' As if from nowhere, I heard myself answer that I jolly well did. The reply was enough for him to dismiss me in utter disgust and he threatened me never to come near his laboratories again. There was little danger of that as far as I was concerned, and I picked up my kit and returned defiantly to the sanctuary of the art room believing that one day I would prove that I could earn a living as an artist. The thrashing did nothing to diminish my enthusiasm for art – in fact, it gave me the resolve to succeed.

Almost twenty-one years later, when I finally became a full-time professional artist, I remembered Archie Goddard and the thrashing he gave me, and the crass ignorance on the part of my school towards the education of the arts. I resolved to telephone the old master and tell him that I had succeeded in becoming a professional artist. He may not have remembered the class-room incident, but I wanted to ring him for the sake of self-satisfaction. Then, that very evening in the local paper, a single column heading stated simply 'School's ex-science chief dies'.

The report caused me to reflect further on the twenty-one swipes and the almost equal number of years that it had taken me to achieve my ambition to paint full-time – one swipe for every year and one for luck.

My fiery dragon, so fearful to an eight-year-old boy and yet so impelling as to inspire that first painting which had been at the root of it all, certainly had more than a little to answer for.

2 A TIME AND A PLACE

Whenever one looks back on the events that have furthered a chosen career, it is obvious that various people and specific places have come together at exactly the right time. My old friend Mrs Read would have said 'It was all in the cards, lad'; others might simply say that it was meant to be. Whether it be luck, fate, chance or divine guidance, however, it does require that the right person is in a particular place at a specific moment in time for the right things to happen. Fortunately for me, such a sequence of events has occurred from time to time over the years, and usually, when they were most needed someone has appeared out of nowhere – or so it seemed – to set in motion a chain of events that would enable me to pursue my passion for painting in one particular direction or another.

It goes without saying that the ability to paint requires a certain talent, but to become a successful artist in the modern world requires in addition the ability to sell oneself, for which self-confidence is a great asset when it comes to meeting people – as well as the acquisition of entrepreneurial skill and business acumen. Above all, however, it is important to maintain a sincerity in one's work without harbouring a conviction that it is God's gift to the art world. The ability to be self-critical is a help in this respect and an awareness of the work of one's contemporaries and peers is always a great leveller and puts one's own abilities and shortcomings in perspective.

On leaving school at the age of sixteen, it was my good fortune to find a job as a trainee display artist and window-dresser. Although painting was merely a hobby – albeit one that I took very seriously – my great desire to make it my profession was still maintained, despite all the advice to the contrary. All my friends in the Leicester Sketch Club, as well as my concerned parents who had no knowledge of the art world, were convinced that it was impossible to earn a living as an artist. However, I was optimistic; after all, were not Terence Cuneo and Edward Seago making a living from art? The fact that they were obviously successful artists gave me hope for the future.

The artists within the Leicester Sketch Club helped to improve my technique and several gave me particular guidance. One was the late Donald Bosher, a member of the Royal Institute of watercolour painters, who produced flourishing watercolours in a fresh, broad style, influenced partly by the work of Seago. We had regular painting trips together and it was a delight to watch him produce as many as two dozen skies in a day. His output was prodigious and his enthusiasm boundless, and occasionally he would produce an outstanding painting.

The Sketch Club had an unofficial off-shoot known as the Saturday group – artists who met each Saturday to paint in the city or out in the countryside. Many were professional commercial artists who worked in advertising agencies and painted as a hobby. Enthusiasm was the keynote for entry into this élite group and if my own work was no match for theirs, my enthusiasm was such that it merited, it seemed, a special welcome. The head of the group was Freddie Wills, as forthright a man as one could ever meet. Physically large, he was convinced of his own infallibility in all matters, called a spade a spade, and would not tolerate either fools or the faint-hearted gladly. A pre-requisite for membership of this inner sanctum of the club was the ability to withstand the most hazardous of weather conditions, for we would go out regardless of the weather. 'Fearless Fred' was as adamant about the weather as he was with everything else. He considered watercolours, for instance, 'namby-pamby', whereas oils were 'the man's medium', and anyone who missed the Saturday afternoon meet because they failed to get through six feet of snow, would be told in no uncertain terms that they had 'no blasted stamina'.

On one unforgettable Saturday when the most bitterly cold wind was blowing, thick ice made road travel inadvisable. Only four out of the nine or ten regular members of the group – Don, Colin, Fred and myself – turned up. 'Where are they all then?' queried Fred, looking at his watch and then at the bus ready to depart for Groby Pool, our destination for the day. 'Don't say they're not coming because of this,' he said with an impatient nod at the ice. 'I think we'll be lucky to see any more today,' Don ventured. 'Rubbish, we are here, aren't we? They've no stamina, that's what's wrong with them,' was Fred's reply.

Fred marched off towards the bus, striding out confidently, as if the ice were not even there. We three gingerly followed. When we were on the bus, Fred continued: 'Damn fools missing out; the light will be great later on; look, it's a lot brighter over there; they've no blasted stamina,' and so it went on, all the way to Groby. I've often thought since that if it weren't for the fact that Freddie was such a good artist, none of us would have tolerated him as we did.

'Princess Alice'
oil painting, 18in × 14in (Jessop Collection)

Cylinder and Valve gear Britannia Class Pacific (pencil sketch)

At Groby we alighted from the bus, cold and with the prospect of worse to come. Fred strode off down the hill towards the frozen pool. The path was treacherous and the three of us slid down after him. At the pool side the light was indeed magnificent, but the wind was biting; it seemed to cut one in half. It was the coldest wind I had ever experienced and I wondered how we were going to paint in such conditions.

Fred obviously felt cold because he turned up his collar and suggested that we went down into a little dell where a frozen stream at the bottom reflected a watery sun through the trees. Don was sent ahead to investigate for subject matter; Fred directed operations from the top of the bank, while Colin and I shivered and watched. Our leader beckoned us down and we negotiated our way down the treacherous path with great care. We were too engrossed in our own progress downwards to notice what happened next, but suddenly we heard a prolonged hapless whine that rose to a terrifying crescendo, the cries coming from Fred who was sitting in a circle of broken ice in the foot-deep waters of the stream. His sodden trilby bobbed up and down in a little pool at his submerged feet. 'Get me out,' he quavered. We immediately obeyed. 'Get me a taxi,' he ordered. Don wrang out Fred's trilby hat and stupidly placed it on his head. The hat drooped ridiculously, mis-shapen and farcical, over Fred's eyes. I stifled my desire to laugh at Fred's dilemma. We helped him up the hill to the bus-stop where fortunately the bus was awaiting its return to the city.

The doors were opened for us by a West Indian conductor who observed with a dazzling display of white teeth and unfortunate hilarity that it had been 'a nice day for a dip in de pool, man'. By this time, Fred was shaking violently, his voice jerking and almost inaudible. I was instructed to sit beside him to keep him warm on the long journey back. Wrapped in Don's coat and with the ridiculous trilby still on his head, Fred shivered all through the return journey to Leicester, a trembling shadow of his former dynamic self.

When we arrived back at the bus station, Fred was like a man possessed. He violently shook the doors to get off the bus while it was still moving, and when it had stopped, he shot across the road like a greyhound out of a trap and skated on the ice to the nearest telephone box where he feverishly made a telephone call. After two unsuccessful attempts to contact his wife, he slammed the telephone down in despair and confessed in an hysterical voice that he had been dialling his Co-op number. We contacted his wife, put him in a taxi, and made our separate ways home under Fred's grave threat of dire consequences if even the slightest whisper about the incident ever reached the other members of the Sketch Club.

Although Freddie is dead, he is well remembered and the stories about him and the rest of that dedicated group of artists are legion. A book could be written about my early days with the Leicestershire art circles whose standards were high and respected nationally, but enough has been written here to demonstrate the dedication that was necessary in pursuit of art.

As to my own dedication at that time, I was totally engrossed in learning all I could about the business of painting by working in both oils and watercolours and occasionally I might earn as much as 2 guineas for my efforts.

By 1957, I was courting Mary and was looking forward to married life. We met in the department store where we both worked and Mary accompanied me on many painting trips, sitting for many hours at my side in all weathers.

Our married life began on a shoe-string budget in a small flat in a rather run-down part of Leicester. It wasn't much of a start but we hoped that things could only get better. My burning desire to paint full-time remained, gnawing away inside me to the extent that I became very dissatisfied with my job and way of life. During the course of the next three years, however, I was promoted to the position of display manager in an outdated department store, and as a result we were able to move to a better flat. In due course, our daughter Karen was born.

The flat had an attic room which soon became a studio. I dressed windows by day, painted in the studio in the evening, met the painting group on Saturdays and took my daughter out in her pram for a short walk as far as the Midland Railway yard on a Sunday. By 1960, when steam was waning, I would turn Karen in her pram towards the lines and from our vantage point overlooking the railway yards below us firmly instruct her to breathe in all that smoke and steam while she had the chance. As a result, she grew up with a total disregard for steam and all its glorious history.

Occasionally, the Saturday group would visit the engine-yard and shed, but whereas I was enormously enthusiastic about capturing the images of the steam shed on canvas, other artists were less keen and they were unable to fully understand my preoccupation with steam as a subject. Eventually, I visited the engine-shed alone. The group's inability to grasp the fact that within a few years there would be no steam engines or steam sheds to paint was a mystery to me.

During the early Sixties I changed my job again – a disastrous mistake – and within six months I was out of work. After looking for employment for a month, the only job I was offered was as a night-duty petrol-pump attendant. Mary insisted that I should not take up the offer but should try producing showcards and label designs. We had no money and were in debt to the grocer and our landlord. We seemed to have reached rock bottom and I tried desperately to get some freelance commercial art work.

During that most difficult year, I scraped a living – earning £5 in a good week, but usually it was only £2 or £3, and some weeks I earned nothing at all. I saw myself as the proverbial artist starving in a garret and I became increasingly depressed. Then, unexpectedly, Mrs Read visited us. She suggested that as Christmas was only three months away, I should produce some hand-painted calendars and she would sell them door-to-door around Leicester. With my high ideals regarding art, I was appalled at the idea of painting mass-produced pictures. However, such was our financial situation, that I reluctantly agreed to do it.

I painted hundreds of calendars and Mary completed them with tabs and ribbon. Each day we worked until it was past midnight making calendars and Mrs Read sold them for half-a-crown (12½p) each. My self-esteem was shattered because I was doing something that I had always insisted I would never do – prostitute my art; I felt that I had totally degraded myself. Then, a month before Christmas, Mrs Read told us that she had exhausted her outlets for the calendars and that she would be busy with her Christmas preparations. She then rummaged in her bag and placed on the table a small Christmas pudding which she hoped we would accept to brighten Christmas day.

It was a well-intentioned gesture, but it seemed like charity, and it prompted me to look for another job. I was employed as a postman for the Christmas period, but the future after that looked as bleak as ever.

Since our marriage, Uncle Harold had moved house and established a tiny draper's business in a lock-up shop in the suburbs of Leicester selling everything from men's caps to industrial overalls and from rugs to ladies' underwear and stockings. Harold visited us the week before Christmas to say he had decided to retire and he wondered if we would like to buy his business. There was little joy for me at the thought of becoming a draper, although Mary's eyes had brightened at the suggestion. However, we had no capital to buy the business, so initially it did not seem to be a viable proposition.

My uncle, it seemed, did not need to be paid for the stock and goodwill immediately, so we could pay him back, he suggested, at the rate of £1 per week from the takings. He told us that we could just make a living from the shop and that I could paint while waiting for customers. So, with that appealing thought, on 1 January 1961 I became a draper and in so doing made the first positive step towards becoming a professional artist – although no one could have foreseen it at the time.

During the quiet patches of mid-week trading, I painted in the tiny back-room and improved my abilities with the brush. The other stroke of good fortune was that the shop was situated next to the railway bank that carried the Midland main line to the North. On many occasions when I glanced out of the window and would see the Thames–Clyde or some lesser working pass by with a dejected Scot or Jubilee at its head, a constant reminder that steam was fast vanishing. Then, as the next few years rolled by, I saw engines travelling past in sad lines behind diesel locomotives. What depressing parades they were; the once mighty were coupled to the humble, some without tenders, some already rusting, others back to front, the empty sound of their connecting rods clanking with a sound like the tolling of a bell. I called them the 'grave-yard specials', and in parting the hand towels and the boiler suits displayed in the shop window, I would often peep out at these trundling processions on their way to the scrapyard at Kettering. The sight of these sad engines stirred my heart, and as a result I made a conscious decision to record as much as possible of what was left before it was too late.

Fate had indeed been kind to me for, by working in that shop at that particular time, it became possible to pursue the task I had set myself. I had a new sense of artistic direction and although I never considered that my work might ever be of any great significance, I realised that I was witnessing the end of a great industrial era, and as an artist I had to record it for posterity.

To my surprise, some customers showed an interest in the paintings on display in the back-room. Pictures of steam engines, it seemed, were of interest to people other than myself despite all the advice I had received to the contrary and occasionally I sold a painting for £8 or £10.

With the advent of the diesel age, another invention – ladies' tights – was to alter the course of my life. The manufacture of ladies' tights heralded the emergence of the supermarket, and their ability to stock huge selections of the articles at a competitive price led to the demise of the draper's corner-shop.

Things looked bleak to say the least. The shop was doomed as far as the sale of drapery was concerned and with three swift strokes of the sword, fate dealt its final blow. Firstly, supermarkets sprang up everywhere, so the day of the corner shop had finally gone; then the industrial overall manufacturers started to sell direct to factories, which halved that side of our business, and

(page 26) 'Carlisle Citadel'
oil painting, 36in × 24in
LMS 4-6-2 'City of St. Albans' leaves Carlisle Citadel with an up express in the autumn of 1947

(page 27) 'Sidelight'
oil painting, 16in × 12in
A golden sunlight glints along the side of No 60137 'Red Gauntlet' at York (Jessop Collection)

thirdly, the council placed a quartet of traffic lights outside the shop so cars could not pull up outside. So we were forced to close and seek another way of earning a living.

The demise of the drapery business gave me an empty shop into which was moved the easel, together with some mouldings and picture-framing equipment. Then some part-time work teaching painting at further education centres came my way. So fate had led me towards a semi-professional existence as an artist, teaching, painting and making picture-frames. The teaching and picture-framing accounted for the best part of our livelihood, but occasionally a painting sold for anything up to £40. The easel near the shop window was seldom without a small audience outside and with my three incomes, we prospered cautiously. We took a mortgage on a Victorian house just outside Leicester and for good measure bought a new bicycle.

Any joy there might have been in this situation was tempered by the long tiring hours I had to work to make a living and the fact that at the end of the day I was still not a full-time professional artist. We could not exist on what

was earned from the sale of pictures, so how could I make it pay enough so that framing and teaching could stop?

Eventually, I made a positive decision to visit art galleries in both London and the provinces to have my work exhibited by one of them. It was the start of a two-year slog that led to the blackest depression I had ever experienced. Not a single person in any of the hundreds of galleries I visited during that period gave me the slightest encouragement. Often they would simply refer me to another gallery nearby. Usually they explained that thousands of artists painted landscapes better than mine and they were unable to make a living. Some would tell me to return with something original, and if steam-engine pictures were included in my collection, they were dismissed as being of no interest to anyone and totally unsaleable. One person who had seen my work shouted to me as I reached the door on my way out: 'Hey, you know what it says on the railway on those iron plates, don't you? It says "Beware of the trains", so I should if I were you.' The taunt made me resolve to buy one of those signs if ever time were to prove him wrong – and now such a sign is fixed to the wall just outside the studio door.

More than the rejection, it was the uncaring off-handed manner that accompanied it that hurt. The provincial galleries were more courteous, but

'Albert Hall' at Tyseley (pencil sketch)

only a few were prepared to display what I had to offer.

After two years of rejection, I began to believe what everyone had been telling me – that to make a living as an artist was impossible. Yet a part of me still clung to the thought that somewhere, some time, I would meet the right person who would enable me to become a successful artist.

It was with this in mind that Mary and I set off for a gallery in York one day in 1968. The gallery's proprietor had seemed genuinely keen to see my work when I telephoned and a firm appointment was made. It was vital that we should save the train fare for two of us to go to York as Mary was concerned about my mental health because by then I was very depressed and her company was welcome. It was fortunate that she was with me because we arrived at the gallery only to find that it had been closed down and was completely empty. In disbelief at our bad luck, we stopped at a café for a coffee and were both near to tears. It had all been a waste of time and money, and yet another hopeful avenue was closed.

As we had a few hours to spare before our train left for home, we decided to visit the old railway museum because it was free and Mary thought that it might just cheer me up. So we wandered between the Ivatt Atlantics and Mr Stirling's beautiful machines in a dejected silence until Mary, suddenly inspired, said, 'Why don't you show your railway paintings to the curator here?' 'Not likely,' was my quick response, 'I've had enough of rejections. I've told you, I've finished with it and that's that.' Our experience in York had been the last straw and I felt that it was time to admit defeat.

Fate then intervened. An attendant overheard our conversation and asked if we would like to see the curator. Before I could refuse, he had fetched Frank Burton, a cheery, smiling man.

Frank Burton shook my hand and said he would be delighted to see my pictures. Nervously, I undid the two bundles which were spread out on and around a chair. 'Oh these are nice,' the curator said, 'Do you do it for a living?' For a second I was speechless, then I explained that I had been trying to become a professional artist for the last twenty years but had been unable to get a start anywhere. 'Well,' said Frank Burton, 'It's no use showing them here; you ought to have them at the British Transport Museum in London. Do you know John Scholes?' John Scholes was the curator of historical records for British Railways Board, but my knowledge of him stretched no further than that. 'I'm going down there tomorrow for a meeting and I'll mention your work to him; he ought to see it. Perhaps he'll give you a ring some time.'

That was the first time that anyone involved in the art gallery or museum world had been enthusiastic about my pictures and it was enough to send us back home feeling a little more optimistic about my prospects. Whether Frank Burton would mention my paintings to John Scholes and whether the great man himself would be interested enough to see them for himself were matters of speculation, but it seemed possible that if one or two of my paintings could be shown at the British Transport Museum, it could be a worthwhile break that might lead to better opportunities.

Being totally honest with myself, I knew that it was futile to think that John Scholes would ever ring me – after all, he was not short of professional artists who wished to hang their work in his gallery. As the weeks went by, my zest for painting waned to the point where it seemed to be futile even to try. One day, when I was feeling particularly depressed, I telephoned the British Transport Museum. I spoke to John Scholes' secretary who was less than forthcoming on the possibility of my seeing her boss until it was mentioned that Frank Burton from York had liked my pictures. Suddenly her attitude changed: Frank Burton had indeed enthused about my pictures and before any more could be said she put me through to Mr Scholes.

I waited with nervous anticipation, my mind filled with a thousand depressing thoughts, until a terse voice asked what I wanted. I replied shakily that I was waiting to speak to Mr Scholes. 'Yes, Scholes here, what do you want?' Taken aback by this aggressive start to our conversation, I explained that I would welcome an interview to show him my work with a view to exhibiting one or two pictures in the museum gallery. He dismissed my request with the reply that only the work of famous artists was exhibited in the gallery – artists such as David Shepherd and Terence Cuneo whose work people would come especially to see. Scholes' bluff, no-nonsense, hard-bitten attitude was immovable and I despaired of meeting this obviously irritable Yorkshireman. As a last resort, I mentioned that Mr Burton had very much liked my paintings, but Scholes' reply was as negative as before: 'Well, that might be so, old man, but you'll be wasting your time and mine. Come back when you've done a bit more. With all due respects to you, old son, nobody's ever heard of you.'

His reply so filled me with frustration that I could barely contain my anger and retorted: 'With all due respects to you, Mr Scholes, if they're all like you and won't even look at my paintings, nobody will ever hear of me.' There was complete silence at the other end of the telephone and I believed that my best opportunity had been lost. Then, in a calmer voice, Scholes said, 'All right, you've got a point there, old son. Now look here, I'll see you next Tuesday at 10.30 sharp. Can you make it? Good, well be here then, but I'm making no promises mind, none at all. I'll just look, right?' And the telephone was slammed down.

Shaking with excitement at what had happened, I realised in glancing at my pictures that there were just six days to improve on the display of pictures propped up around me. Suddenly, there was the drive and all the ambition in the world to do something that in some measure would compare with the work of the two artists Scholes had mentioned. Their names echoed in my head; they were, after all, at the top of their profession whereas I had not even had one professional exhibition. However, I was not going to let this chance evade me.

Five days later, after working well into the night each day, I had completed three oils which were definitely an improvement on my past standard. I was so exhausted by my efforts, though, that I could not imagine how they would be received.

One thing was absolutely certain, however: this was to be my final push for a career as a professional artist. If John Scholes rejected me, I would abandon my ambition.

3 EVERY PICTURE
TELLS A STORY

John Scholes was an enigma, a man of moods, gregarious one minute, downcast or aggressive the next. His appearance and bluff manner belied his position as the head of the British Transport Museum. In that building he had built up a magnificent collection of historical relics from great locomotives to railway teaspoons and from royal rolling-stock to paintings. He had a considerable liking for paintings and an extensive knowledge to back it up; over the years he had purchased many paintings for the collection, not only by artists from the past but also from the famous names that he had met along the way.

The journey to the city was a tense one and Mary fully understood how important it was to me to come back with something – anything, as long as there was some hope for the future.

At the museum Mary and I separated, she to spend the time looking around while I met Mr Scholes. At a minute to half-past ten I was shown into a large room with an ancient board-room table down its length; at one end of the room was the door to the secretary's office and at the other was a door marked 'Scholes'. His secretary emerged to greet me. 'He'll not keep you long, dear,' she said smilingly, 'I'll just tell him you are here.' From within the Scholes door, a belligerent voice bellowed 'Who?' The secretary came out, the same fixed smile almost in place, and returned to her office. She then emerged with a sheaf of paper in her hand and went to Scholes' office, but she almost ran out backwards as a shirt-sleeved arm scattered her paper into the air. 'I've told you, woman, I don't want anything more to do with these idiots. I've had more than enough.' The door slammed shut, while she was on her knees picking up the scattered letters, assuring me that Scholes would be all right soon. The secretary rose to walk towards her office, hesitated, and in a confidential tone said, 'Only he breeds lurchers, you know,' she nodded across to the other side of the room where a basket lay in the corner, 'He brought that bitch in this morning to be mated and it got out, and a mongrel's had it, so that's why he's a bit sharp.'

It was difficult to believe what was happening and I was passing from the terrified stage into a state of numbed disbelief that I was there at all. Then suddenly Scholes himself appeared. 'Mr Webster?' 'No,' I said, 'Weston.' 'Well, whatever it is, I told you on the phone it's no use you coming here; I only want famous artists at the top of the tree. Anyway, now you're here, I'll have a look because I said I would, but don't expect anything.' Pointing to the long table he said, 'Prop them up along there. I'm going for a fag. I'll be back in a minute.'

My hands untied the two bundles and shakily propped them up along the length of the table. As my eyes viewed that line of pictures, they suddenly looked quite awful to me; every picture had glaring errors that I should have noticed before they had left the easel.

John Scholes reappeared, a cigarette drooping casually from his lip. Without a word, he slowly walked along the line of paintings. At the top end, he gave me a glance and came back to the first one, progressing along the line more slowly than before. The entire process was done in total silence. On reaching the last picture in the line, he looked at me long and hard. I felt like a condemned man awaiting the death sentence. Scholes then said quietly, 'You didn't tell me you could paint like this.' I told him that they represented my standard to date and that although I was aware that I hadn't yet reached the heights of a Cuneo or a Shepherd, I did have hopes for the future. 'Well, young man,' he said, advancing towards me with his hand outstretched, 'You're good enough for me. What do you want – a one-man show? Three months – is that all right for you?' My mind was in a whirl, but John Scholes was already planning the show. 'Is March 1969 to the following June all right? Come on, I'll show you my gallery. We've got David Shepherd's stuff in there at present and you'll need about the same – thirty paintings, unframed. I have my own way of showing them against black felt.' We did a whirlwind tour of the gallery. 'It's got to be right, David. I shall promote you as "my discovery" and I'll make sure the right people come along to see your pictures.'

A door had been opened and through it lay a very different future for Mary and myself. At that moment, of course, I couldn't see how, only the bright light of optimism at the thought of a London showing and in such a prestigious gallery. But above the excitement was the conviction that I was living through a day that would change my life, and when Mary eventually caught up with me, she too was overjoyed at my news.

The moment that was a major turning point in my life was at about 11 o'clock on a Tuesday in September 1968: one man in the right place at the

'Blue Peter at York'
oil painting, 40in × 30in
One of the paintings from the 1969 exhibition at The British Transport Museum

The Coaling Plant at Leicester engine yard. This oil painting (48in × 36in) was the centrepiece of my 1969 exhibition at The British Transport Museum

right time. John Scholes had become the first of the men in my life who played an important role in forming my career as a full-time painter.

The exhibition at the British Transport Museum proved to be everything that I could ever have wished for. Almost all the paintings were sold and in addition I was given a commission list of well over a year's work. The exhibition also gave me the chance to put my prices up to over the £100 mark, which in 1969 seemed remarkable. I had some good press and television coverage too, to make the public aware of the show's existence.

At last I was on my way, the corner had been turned, and many pleasant things were about to happen as a result. I well remember the glow I felt on seeing for the first time my name on a poster in a tube station: 'David Weston, the railway artist – a John Scholes discovery', and a letter that came from the office of the Chairman of ICI, Sir Peter Allen, inviting me to show him my work. He bought two at that time and has added to his collection since. There are memories too of the day John rang to say that he had someone at the museum who wanted to buy a picture or two. It was The Hon. William McAlpine, the industrialist, who not only bought three paintings from the show but commissioned a further six. I also received unexpectedly a letter from Terence Cuneo, whom I had not met at that time, saying that he had visited the exhibition. That letter is still among my souvenirs of the exhibition. In it he wrote:

I think it is excellent, you have a fine feeling for the gallant old iron horse. I particularly enjoyed your atmospheric studies, particularly the one next Scholes' office door (sold) of an almost head-on view. I like too the restraint of your palette in many of the canvases, the true, almost monochromatic atmosphere one gets around loco sheds and coaling plants . . . I told friend Scholes that I thought it was a damn Good Exhibition!

Such rewards after the years of rejection were sweet indeed, and of course the success meant that it was possible for me to give up teaching and pass on the framing business to my father, who ran it successfully until he retired some years later.

To the world outside who knew nothing of my years of struggle, I had turned professional 'overnight'. My pictures were still being produced in the little premises next to the railway line but with the framing business moved to next door, they had taken on much more the appearance of a studio.

My easel was invariably placed near the window and many regulars popped in for a chat and a look at what was on the easel. One of these regulars was old Phil Brown who must have bored all his friends talking about my paintings. He suffered from bad eyesight and wore thick bulbous glasses and a brown trilby hat. Whenever Phil examined one of my pictures he usually started at the bottom with his face only inches away from the wet canvas and slowly went up to the top, the brim of his trilby missing the wet oil paint by no more than a whisker. I always watched him anxiously, transfixed at the closeness of the brim preceding his field of vision. Then, one day while I was in the back

room making a cup of tea, Phil said that he liked my painting on the easel but he wanted to know why I had left a broad stripe of canvas up the middle. A glance at his trilby revealed the answer, for it sported a thick dollop of oil paint on the front edge of its brim. I couldn't tell him the truth.

Customers for my paintings varied enormously and it was not only professional people and the wealthy who beat a path to my door. One man withdrew all his savings to buy a painting the week before he was due to get married. He admitted that he was terrified at what his bride-to-be might say and although I did not find out, the painting was not returned.

One day a worker from the foundry nearby came to the studio. He was wearing a greasy cap and carried his flask and sandwich tin in a little leather bag. He nodded at a very large painting at the back of the studio of two great Northern engines on shed. 'I likes that, master, it's arlreet is that,' he said and shuffled his feet in an embarrassed fashion. 'You don't mind if I have a look at it, do you?' 'Of course not,' I said. 'That's what they are there for; look as much as you like.' He looked long and hard in silence for several minutes, then said, ''Ow much would a thing like that cost then, master?' '£150, sir,' was my firm reply. 'Oh you beauty, master, I ain't got that sort o' money, but I do like it. Would it be all right if I come in again to have another look?' I assured him sincerely that of course it would.

The next evening the man visited me again. He nodded at me and stood in silence again before the painting. Then he asked me to repeat the price. I told him the same figure as before, at which he took the sandwich tin slowly out of his bag and asked me to count out 150 £1 notes. 'I can't get it out of me mind, you see, so I've decided I'm going to have it.'

As the painting was so large, it had to be delivered to the little terraced house in which he lived. 'Can you bring it through into the parlour, master? I want it up there behind the piano.' Quickly estimating the available space, I could see at a glance that the lower third of the painting would drop below the height of the piano. Having pointed this out, however, it didn't seem to bother the foundry-worker. 'There ain't nowhere else for it, master. Hang it up.' That done, we stood back to view the result. As predicted, one third of the painting dropped behind the piano, but the next foot was viewed through a selection of old newspapers, tins, Guinness bottles, a lamp, old books and two pot dogs. I was flabbergasted and suggested that we should clear away all the clutter. 'Good God, no, master it will all be back on there as soon as you'd gone out the door.' He sighed a contented sigh and said, 'Great, ain't it, master, and worth every penny.'

From that little studio it was as important for me to learn how to be a businessman as it was to improve on my painting technique. It had been my good fortune to be introduced into the society of a wealthy clientele through the ever-widening net of introductions from my London exhibition, so learning the right manners for such company became a necessity.

Within two years the turn-around in our fortunes meant that we could look for a better home for ourselves. We found what we were looking for in an eighteenth-century cottage with a stable block and paddock at the rear.

*Alan Bloom and myself in pensive mood inside the shed at Bressingham Steam Museum (*East Anglian Times*)*

A part of the stable block was suitable for conversion into a new studio, and as Karen was interested in ponies, the property was perfect for our personal needs as well as suitable for future development as my career blossomed.

While I was working for the London exhibition, it had been our pleasure to go for the first time, in December 1968, to Bressingham in Norfolk, to paint a picture of the Britannia Pacific *Oliver Cromwell*, and through this we began a friendship with Alan and Flora Bloom that we value to this day. Bressingham Steam Museum was then in its infancy; Alan had just built a large engine-shed with no more than a chance that British Rail would allow any of their preserved locomotives to go there. The problem was that without a shed British Rail would never agree to any of its main-line engines going there, but for Alan to build the shed without a firm guarantee could have spelt financial disaster for the Blooms. And an empty shed with no main-line engines would not have attracted the paying public through the museum gates.

The fact that Alan took such a gamble is typical of this man who frequently walked the tight-rope between success and disaster in his quest to build Bressingham gardens and his beloved steam museum into a centre of national importance.

Author and horticulturist of world acclaim, Alan Bloom created the gardens at Bressingham originally as a hobby related to his established nursery business. His delightful dell garden is picturesque at all times of the year, but when one realises that he created this little masterpiece almost single-handed, from the beautiful island beds and pond to the construction of a thatched brick and flint shelter, and the even more remarkable little bridge which he built in the winter months by the light of his car headlamps, then one begins to understand the measure of the man.

With the increasing number of visitors to the gardens, steam came to Bressingham. In 1961 Alan's first traction engine was bought with a view to its restoration and others quickly followed. The engines proved to be a popular attraction to visitors, so steam began to be a feature of the open days at the gardens and the seeds were sown for the establishment of the magnificent collection of road and rail locomotives that exists at Bressingham today.

We watched with interest as the museum developed, continually being amazed at Alan's energy and resourcefulness. If track needed to be laid, then he would do it whatever the weather – narrow gauge or standard gauge, almost every sleeper has passed through Alan's hands – if a water well needed to be dug, Alan would dig it himself. Now an octogenerian, he is still as tough and energetic as ever. He still works the same long hours as before and it is often the case that if you want to have a conversation with him you must go down to the potting shed to do it.

It was in 1970 that Alan and I made a trip to Germany together. For me it was a chance to draw something of live steam in action and on shed. For Alan the main reasons for the trip were to buy a narrow gauge engine for the 2ft gauge 'nursery line', and to assess the possibilities of purchasing a 2-10-0 freight engine to broaden the scope of his collection.

We found an 0-6-0 Orenstein and Koppel for the narrow gauge which Alan secured a deal on, but it later proved to be too heavy and of too long a wheel-base for the tight curves of the Bressingham circuit; it spread the rails which caused its train of coaches to derail, so eventually it had to go.

Of the freight engines in Germany at that time there was an abundance of the 2-10-0 class 50s and at Hamburg we were entertained royally and given the freedom to wander at will in the yards and round-house, with the occasional opportunity to ride on the foot-plate as well.

The aggressive design of the massive 50s and the class 94 tank locomotives formed the basis of most of my sketches at Hamburg, but the tremendous size of the 012 class Pacific oil-burners at the Altona shed was awe-inspiring;

'Sunlight at Hamburg'
oil painting, 16in × 12in
*German class 50s in steam during 1970 (*Jessop Collection*)*

the shed and turn-table there made a wonderful backdrop to these Teutonic giants.

The purchase of a German locomotive was not straightforward because the Germans phased out steam very gradually (and wisely), so only run-down engines were offered for sale; the huge overhaul costs that would have been entailed, together with the shipping costs, would have made the total price prohibitive. With this in mind, we caught the train to Denmark where we viewed lines of redundant engines that had only just come out of service. Alan could find nothing suitable and there was little time for sketching as we had only a matter of hours before our ferry departed for England. However, I photographed what interested me and several canvases resulted from the few hours we spent in Denmark.

In 1975, Alan acquired from the Norwegian government a German Keieglok class locomotive that had been walled up in a tunnel by the NATO authorities in 1953. When the tunnel was reopened in 1968 the engine was found to be in perfect working order. It has joined the forty or more engines at Bressingham, including the Coronation class Pacific *Duchess of Sutherland* and the rebuilt *Royal Scot*, both freed from the captivity of Butlin's holiday camps and now restored to their former glory by the excellent team of engineers and fitters in the Bressingham workshops.

To be seated in Bressingham's gardens on a summer's day with the smells and sounds of steam engines and the music from Flora's splendid set of golden gallopers is a delightful experience, one of gaiety and colour, but the Bressingham I love best is when the crowds have gone for the season and I can stroll down by the lake and along the track-bed into the fen with a sketchbook and pencils or settle down quietly in a corner of the barn, as I did to produce a picture of the Hudswell-Clarke engine *Bronwllydd* that was being rebuilt for the summer season.

For Alan, there is nothing he likes better than to ride on the foot-plate of one of his little Penrhyn locomotives as it trundles its way around the nursery line on a busy open day. I've enjoyed that experience beside him many times over the years and have often wondered how many thousands of circuits he has driven. But as his eyes scan his beloved acres, you can be sure that he will be thinking about a new scheme, a new plant to propagate, a new book to write, or a new engine to acquire or restore. No matter where one looks at Bressingham, from the nurseries to the gardens or the steam museum, while acknowledging the enormous amount achieved by Alan's two sons, and the family and staff, one cannot escape the unmistakable stamp of 'the governor's' hand: it's as clear as any signature on a painting.

The Bressingham Museum has, of course, been the venue for three of my exhibitions: more recently, the 'Jessop Collection' exhibition, which will be described in detail later, was shown throughout the summer season of 1988, and prior to that the set of paintings on the development of the English traction engine enjoyed a season's showing, as did the twenty-four paintings that were done for Bill McAlpine on the story of the British steam locomotive.

Bill McAlpine's interest and enthusiasm for steam are, of course, legendary.

His private museum has a magnificent collection of models, paintings and relics, as well as a number of full-size traction engines and locomotives. His liking of paintings of the steam age has led him to build up a collection of works by most of the leading artists in the field, and the patronage he gave to me in the early years of my professional career was extraordinary.

Bill bought dozens of my pictures for his home, museum and London offices, in addition to the commissions I received from his company for such diverse subjects as power stations under construction, a shopping complex in Edinburgh and the construction of concrete oil-rigs on the Clyde. One painting was a large oil of the Forth Bridge which was hung in his London office. One afternoon Bill rang me at the studio to tell me that as the afternoon light changed towards evening, so it became darker on the painting. It was a small detail but I appreciated the fact that such a busy man should contact me about it.

In finding expression for his own interest in steam, Bill McAlpine has done a considerable amount for those who have made their livelihood from either the preservation movement or model-making, or for artists like Barry Clark who received considerable patronage from Bill following in my own footsteps. Bill's saving of the *Flying Scotsman* from a disastrous fate in the USA after its ill-fated tour of that country is a legend in the story of the British preservation movement. Without Bill McAlpine that famous locomotive might have been lost forever to this country. But now its regular appearances have given pleasure to the thousands who have travelled behind her, or simply watched from the line-side.

Bill's enthusiasm knows no bounds, for in the grounds of his home, tucked away in a corner by the museum, is a full-size country station, complete throughout, with a tunnel and a working signal-box. An 0-6-0 saddle-tank locomotive can often be heard barking up the steep bank towards the station. Again, for those enthusiasts among his many friends this is indeed a great treat and one which Bill unselfishly shares with others who can only look in admiration and perhaps a little envy at this remarkable little complex.

The interest that Bill showed in my work during the early Seventies did much to ensure a more secure future for Mary and myself. Commissions were coming in from many sources, but it became apparent that I needed the security of a long-term commitment so that I could see just a few years ahead instead of having to trust that the offers for single commissions would continue.

At the end of my first year as a professional artist, the one year's work had turned into two and that in due course became three, and so on. That happy position was maintained, but I wanted to create something more than simple pictures of the steam age; an interesting story of the entire era existed, from the pioneers and the great Victorians, to the engines of the Thirties – the

Working pencil drawing for 'Winter in the Barn, Bressingham'

'Sid's Roller' Bressingham 1970

Sid's Roller at Bressingham.

zenith of steam – and then to the dismal ending in the breakers' yards of the Sixties. I felt that there must be a way to depict a little of this great story on canvas.

At first my ideas were disjointed; odd canvases would suggest themselves, but overall the vast range of events over one hundred and fifty years of history was distilling in my mind. Should I concentrate on the engines, and what about the companies and their architecture; what of the chief mechanical engineers? Could they be represented? And out of all that history and progress how could one get it down to, say, two dozen canvases? I mulled over all these questions and eventually a pattern began to emerge. The entire project would consist of twenty-four large canvases that would show all those aspects in multi-image form, each canvas depicting a railway company or period in time. The whole was to be a logical sequence of events and developments that would show the rise and fall of the age of steam in Great Britain.

The knowledge that the project would have to be sponsored concerned me because I had never tried to sell anything so large before and I wondered whether someone would pay the amount of money needed to do it and whether they would be patient enough to wait for the three or four years that it would take, allowing for the fact that other work had to be done.

Eventually, it seemed logical to talk to John Scholes about these ideas. His enthusiasm was instant. 'You must do it David,' he said, 'It will make you famous,' and he explained that such an exhibition would be unique because no one had ever done anything like it before. However, he made it plain that his Museum could not think of sponsorship because there were plans for its closure and removal to the newly envisaged National Railway Museum. Even John's future was in the balance and he showed a great, if unnecessary, concern that even if he was asked to take on the directorship of the new museum, he would not be able to do it justice.

It was concern over John's future that caused Bill McAlpine to invite him to have lunch with him at the Dorchester Hotel during 1972. The invitation was extended to myself and it was one that I was very happy to accept. Conversation that day ranged from John's problems to the plans for the new museum at York. John then brought up the subject of my plans for a history of steam on canvas. Bill's reaction was as enthusiastic as John's had been, and after some thought, he decided that he would sponsor it himself, with the payments due, as I envisaged, over a five-year period.

It was to be an on-going project of considerable proportions, a challenge for me to meet, and at the same time the guaranteed payments for the following five years was a good basis to build each year's income on – a measure of security that is a luxury in the art world.

'Winter in the Barn, Bressingham'
oil painting, 18in × 14in
Bronwllydd, the Hudswell-Clarke is rebuilt in the aged and cluttered barn. The light and conglomeration of bits and pieces create the atmosphere of this busy interior (Jessop Collection)

In retrospect, that meeting with Bill McAlpine proved to be a second turning point in my life because it was the start of things to come in terms of similar-sized projects on different subjects for other sponsors. It was, in fact, the start of a way of working that was to set the pattern for years to come.

By the time the last of the paintings for the project was completed, I began to feel concerned at how they might be received by the public because they were different from anything I had previously produced. Bill was enthusiastic about the content and the concept of the show, as were my friends, but to me that was of little encouragement. The project had left me exhausted due to the mental effort that I had put into the series, together with an overloaded order book for other paintings on a variety of subjects. However, the time had come to exhibit the work, so, together with some friends, we started to look for a suitable London venue.

Eventually, the Royal Exchange in the heart of the City of London, which then had an excellent exhibition concourse, agreed to an exhibition. A large area was needed because there were 135ft of linear canvas when the paintings were displayed side by side, and as the story read from left to right as in a book it was essential that they were displayed to be viewed consecutively from painting No 1. The Royal Exchange proved to be perfect for this, allowing the entire run of canvases to be shown in a straight line.

During the first two or three days of the exhibition in July 1977 a few hundred people had visited it, some because they had wandered in, as happens with all exhibitions, and others as a result of the press and Midlands television who had given the show good coverage. Relatively few people, however, spoke to me about the paintings, so it was difficult to judge how well they were being received. Then a timely stroke of luck occurred when Mary rang me at the exhibition to say that the television programme *Nationwide* wanted to cover the show and would I please ring them. The following evening I was given a seven-minute interview with Valerie Singleton and illustrated our conversation with many of my paintings. I felt that the interview had gone well and decided to stay in London to see what effect this popular television programme at peak viewing time might have on the number of visitors coming to the exhibition.

The results the next day were unbelievable, for as soon as the doors opened at 10 o'clock, people poured in and by lunchtime they were four or five deep along the whole length of the paintings, studying them and reading the notes at the side of each one. There was a continuous queue of people waiting to shake my hand and to tell me which was their favourite picture or to ask why a certain thing had been done in a certain way. The congratulations were overwhelming and it became obvious that the paintings were a success with the public. At lunchtime, the chief constable of the Royal Exchange struggled excitedly through the crowd to tell me that there had been over three thousand visitors and that he had never seen such crowds before in all his years there.

As my eyes scanned the line of people viewing my work so intently, those at the back struggling to get in closer, I was filled with emotion. One visitor was an elderly Cockney woman who was convinced that one of my paintings

Canvas No 19 'Staniers Giants' (60in × 60in) from the History of the British Steam Locomotive Collection

was of the very engine that her late husband had driven; another was a Midland region driver in uniform, with tears in his eyes, who said, 'I was all right mate 'til I got to those last three in the scrapyards and that done me'; then, in total contrast, there was an elderly city man in pinstripes and a bowler hat who solemnly shook my hand and said, 'I shall not apologise for these tears, sir, but they are the most moving set of paintings I have ever set eyes on. It is a privilege to be here.' He turned and vanished into the crowd. Such compliments and genuine reactions were the only answer I needed to know that my quest had not been in vain, whatever the art world might think about paintings of railways as being of little account.

After all my doubts and fears, the exhibition's success was sweet indeed and the news soon travelled to the office of my sponsor, Bill McAlpine. How I wished that he had been there that day to see the visitors' reactions. However, he told me that his intention was to throw a celebratory party at the exhibition one evening towards the end of its run at the Royal Exchange. That party was a huge success for all concerned and convinced Bill that a nationwide tour of the paintings was possible, so the exhibition was duly organised to appear

at museums as far apart as the Royal Scottish Museum in Edinburgh, the National Museum of Wales in Cardiff and the Ulster Museum of Transport in Belfast. Undoubtedly one of the highlights of its four-year tour was the nine months' run the show enjoyed at the National Railway Museum where a gallery was specially adapted to show the paintings.

My only regret over the exhibition's tour was that John Scholes had not lived to see it, for I know he would have rejoiced in it and taken an impish pleasure in telling everyone that he had 'discovered' me.

John died in 1974 some time after a start had been made on the series. He had been the Curator of Historical Relics for British Railways Board since 1951 and had ensured through his efforts the preservation of steam locomotives well before any private individuals or preservation societies had taken a real interest.

Among my souvenirs is an invitation from the McAlpines to a farewell party at the British Transport Museum on 17 April 1973. We were there, but the party was not all fun for John; he never came to terms with the final closure of his beloved museum and as a result suffered a nervous breakdown from which he never recovered.

There were further joys, however, to come from the showing of the McAlpine pictures and the greatest was an invitation to Buckingham Palace to talk to His Royal Highness Prince Philip, The Duke of Edinburgh, about the series. Bill was naturally invited to join me for what turned out to be an easy and informal discussion in the splendour of the prince's study. His Royal Highness discussed the paintings at some length but was also interested in the concept of industry and business sponsorship of the arts. That was in 1977 and it has now, of course, become a theme pursued by the government of the day. It is something which has also become essential to me in the production of further series of paintings on subjects as diverse as the story of the British motor car sponsored by ISF Ltd, and the development of the English country house sponsored by businessman Mr Trevor Bennett.

The Jessop Collection is another example of this concept in action. This exhibition comprises a collection of forty of my railway paintings and forty complementary photographs by that extraordinary artist with a camera, Colin Garratt. It is a show that is currently on tour following in the footsteps of my previous exhibitions.

Colin's path first crossed with mine in 1969, prior to my exhibition at the British Transport Museum. A friend of mine, Richard Willis, had made a half-hour film about my activities as a painter of the steam age called 'Steam, Oils and Canvas' which was due to be shown concurrently with the BTM exhibition, but with John Scholes' permission we decided to hold a public preview evening in Leicester where both the film and the paintings were to be shown. Colin was in the audience that evening and sought me out afterwards to tell me how much his photographs echoed my own visual interpretations of the steam years.

At that time Colin was as unknown a photographer as I was a painter, and he was particularly anxious to get a first book of his pictures published. Some weeks after, we met again at my home to view a selection of his slides, which confirmed our thoughts that our coincidence of vision was rather remarkable, from content and composition to atmosphere, light and colour.

We met only occasionally after that, but some time later I was delighted to read of his success in the publication of his first book and that more were to follow as his self-imposed task of recording the last vestiges of world steam on film progressed. Colin's journeys worldwide and my own busy professional life as a painter kept us apart and it was sixteen years before we were to meet again.

It was an article in a newspaper about Colin's pictures that prompted me to think that we should renew our friendship. However, the following week he rang me unexpectedly and the result was a pleasant evening in the studio reminiscing. I was soon thinking about a joint exhibition because, despite the intervening years, our pictures still had many parallels. A joint exhibition not only seemed to be a natural outcome of our creativity, but it would spur me into painting some of the subjects from my sketches that I had done many years ago and that had never been touched. We decided to make the theme of the show the 'atmosphere' of the steam era, with the accent on light and mood rather than the nuts and bolts of locomotive portraiture.

Colin responds to the atmosphere of the railway scene as I do – you won't find many 'nuts' and 'bolts' in either Colin's pictures or mine. We are not picture-making simply for the sake of recording fact – important though that is for some – but in trying to capture the essence of what we see in engines and railways, we both work to produce an image that is a work of art first and foremost, one that will hopefully appeal to everyone, whether they are interested in railways or not.

When we finally assembled the pictures that would eventually comprise 'The Jessop Collection', it was interesting to find that a composition which Colin had photographed in an Indian scrapyard was uncannily like a scene painted at Cohen's scrapyard at Kettering. Another of a British engine working the molten waste tippers in Turkey was almost identical to my own sighting and painting at Stewart's and Lloyd's Corby works in Northamptonshire. One of his photographs, taken looking into the light of an Indian dawn, had an enormous affinity with my painting under similar lighting and colour at Merthyr Vale colliery in South Wales. That affinity between our pictures was demonstrated repeatedly and it came to form the axis of the show.

I'm not sure whether a photographer and an artist have ever combined to exhibit together before – certainly it has not been done in the field of railway art – and doubtless it would not be so now were it not for the sponsorship given to us by Jessop's, the photographic retailers. The obvious connections with photography combined with the fact that the company's chairman, Alan Jessop, had been acquiring my steam paintings for a great many years, made the company a prime target for an approach, and so in due course The Jessop Collection became a reality.

In order that a good balance was maintained between the photographs and the paintings, the size of my canvases was kept down to below 20 ×

16in – these smaller sizes were also more suitable for many of the subjects that I planned to paint from my old sketches, some of them no more than a quick scribble in adverse conditions, but enough to evoke a vivid memory of a particular moment in time: a moonlit night on the canal in Leicester when I was sent on my way by a suspicious policeman who would not believe my explanation that I wanted to draw the scene under the light of a bicycle lamp; the derelict signal box on the old Great Northern where my efforts to draw were ultimately defeated by the wetness of the paper; a rather lonely tank-engine in an engine-yard increasingly becoming lost in the snow, or the contrasts of rich, warm and cool colours on rusting wheels as they caught the light between the weeds at Barry.

Colin's photographs hang alongside my paintings, the two art forms blending together with an extraordinary ease, yet one would never think of my painting technique as a photographic one. Colin's thoughts on this are expressed in his piece for the exhibition catalogue:

My concern is with the wonderment of the legend in all its animated diversity; a rusted hulk languishing in a jungle graveyard festooned with tropical blooms is just as exciting to me as a 200 ton giant high-balling across the landscape with a 2,000 ton train. After all, we know the locomotive's technical characteristics, such details are secure for all time. It is the emotive and atmospheric aspects to which future generations will most respond.

I would like to think that my paintings of the steam era echo all aspects of this wide-ranging subject; certainly, the personal reflections of The Jessop Collection form a different conception from the McAlpine pictures on the story of the British steam locomotive, but that was produced over a decade ago and an artist must never stand still with regard to improving his technique. Ideas and conceptions must develop alongside the improvement of one's technique whilst at the same time accepting that the 'perfect' picture is never going to be painted. In the painter's eyes, the elusive masterpiece will never be done and in the forty years that I have been painting on canvas, I have never produced one picture that I was 100 per cent happy with, and hopefully, never will, because it is constant self-criticism and the striving to improve that drives one forward with renewed vigour to the next painting and the next project.

(page 42) '1941 and Britain at War'
oil painting, 50in × 50in
A wartime montage showing Bulleids Pacifics – from The History of the British Steam Locomotive Collection

(page 43) 'Wheels and Weeds'
oil painting, 12in × 10in
*Rich colour and textures at Barry (*Jessop Collection*)*

MR. O.V.S. BULLEID'S "REVOLUTIONARY"
PACIFIC LOCOMOTIVE OF 1941
THE "MERCHANT NAVY" CLASS.

1941

IN WAR AND PEACE
WE SERVE

GWR · LMS · LNER · SR

BULLEID'S "BATTLE OF BRITAIN" CLASS.
INTRODUCED IN 1946
21C151 "WINSTON CHURCHILL"

4 OF PAINTERS AND PAINTINGS

The railway art movement started in earnest at the beginning of the 1970s, following the demise of the steam locomotive.

During the late Sixties, only a small number of artists had recorded the steam age, but before then few had considered steam locomotives as either suitable or exciting material for pictures.

During the mid-nineteenth century, following the construction of the railways in Victorian England, railways had been drawn and painted by some reputable artists. Among them was John C. Bourne, a superb draughtsman, who recorded in accurate graphic detail the construction of railways by the navvies and the simplicity of the equipment that was used to move into place manually huge blocks of granite. Bourne's beautiful pictures of the Great Western Railway between Paddington and Bristol reflect the Victorians' love of nature because the bridges, viaducts and even stations were designed painstakingly to blend into the surrounding countryside in an unobtrusive manner. By 1846 Bourne's glorious interpretations of Wharncliffe Viaduct and the bridges at Maidenhead and Basildon, graphically illustrated this careful blending of man's work with the landscape; it is also reflected in his drawing of Box tunnel and the entry into Bath through the rural charm of 'Bath Hampton' and 'St James's Bridge and Station' in Bath, which are depicted in the most beautiful blend of line, tone and detail on the one hand, while emphasising the enhancement of the natural landscape by the Great Western Railway's architectural delights on the other.

John Bourne saw nothing to offend his artistic eye with the introduction of the railway into the landscape – even his steam locomotives sidle along smiling like some early 'Thomas the tank engine', their smoke sifting gently out of their high chimneys anxious not to disturb the peace of a Victorian landscape.

During the 1830s, a decade or so before Bourne was drawing the Great Western Railway, J. W. Carmichael and T. T. Bury were producing engravings that showed the new railways developing. Their work was not as spectacular or accomplished as Bourne's, but it nonetheless reflected the growth of railway construction that had virtually taken a hold of England at that time, for by 1844 an unprecedented number of 220 bills to sanction new lines was put before parliament.

In May of the same year the Royal Academy opened its doors for its annual exhibition and showed among its many exhibits a painting by J. M. W. Turner entitled 'Rain, Steam and Speed: The Great Western Railway'. Compared to J. C. Bourne's serene perspectives of the railway, Turner's explosive composition was in direct contrast; here the artist made an aggressive and dramatic impact with his engine almost like a fireball battling with the elements, a black and fearful form that was a threat to nature rather than something in sympathy with it.

Turner's painting was not intended to be a record of the Great Western Railway in the way that Bourne's pictures were. Turner's vision was depiction of the railway's atmosphere as well as a portrayal of the dramatic battle with the forces of nature.

J. M. W. Turner had as many critics as he had admirers and an extract from an article in *The Times* of 8 May 1844 read:

> . . . The railways have furnished Turner with a new field for the exhibition of his eccentric style. His 'Rain, Steam and Speed' shows the Great Western in a very sudden perspective, and the dark atmosphere, the bright sparkling fire of the engine, and the dusky smoke, form a very striking combination. Whether Turner's pictures are dazzling unrealities, or whether they are realities seized upon at a moment's glance, we leave his detractors and admirers to settle between them.

To many people 'Rain, Steam and Speed' is a work of genius, although my preference is for Turner's shipping and seascapes where one senses a greater knowledge of the anatomy of his subject.

In France during the latter part of the nineteenth century, the impressionist Claud Monet also looked to the railways for inspiration with the painting of the 'Railway Bridge at Argenteuil' (1875) and the better known 'Gare St Lazare' series of paintings (1877). In England, others found painterly material within the confines of the railway station, William Frith's interpretation being perhaps better known than most, but for the following fifty or sixty years the railway was only rarely considered a suitable subject for the artist's brush.

Cuthbert Hamilton Ellis, better known originally as an author of railway subject matter, began to paint trains simply for pleasure. Ellis' early memories of the London South Western go back as far as 1911, but it was his book *The Trains We Loved*, illustrated with his pictures and published in 1947, that promoted him as a painter of the railway scene. The book was followed by others that used the paintings he had produced for pleasure.

The almost child-like approach of an Ellis watercolour, with its hard landscape and polished engines and train, depict the trains of yesteryear, an idyllic existence in which grime and dirt play no part, and even the smoke is for the best part white.

The work of C. Hamilton Ellis has enormous charm and, within the confines of a naïve technique, the accuracy of his detail reflects his deep knowledge of the subject. There is a distinct link between this painter and that other artist whose passion for railways led him towards recording the railway scene as far back as the Thirties and Forties, Terence Cuneo. It was a series of books to be published by the Oxford University Press that brought Cuneo and Ellis together. Ellis would write the text and Cuneo was to produce the drawings. Through this working arrangement the two men became friends, and as Hamilton Ellis admired the drawings so much, he purchased most of the originals from the publisher.

It was in 1948 that Terence Cuneo was first commissioned by British Railways to do a series of posters depicting various aspects of the railway scene, the first of which was 'Giants Refreshed' showing an A4 and an A2 resplendent in their fresh liveries within the paint-shops at Doncaster. It was soon followed by such memorable pictures as 'Clear Road Ahead', a foot-plate view on a Great Western Castle, and 'An Engine is Wheeled' which graphically illustrated an engine being lowered onto its wheels at Derby works.

For Cuneo, railways had been a passion since childhood, but a serious interest in oil painting did not begin until 1936 when he was twenty-nine years old. Prior to that, he had worked as a commercial illustrator, but although his work in oils over the next few decades depicted an immense variety of subject matter, railways (the British rail posters apart) did not feature largely in his output or commission list until the Sixties.

One other painter of note who had painted steam in the Fifties was David Shepherd. During 1955, Shepherd had painted at Willesden, York and Swindon, depicting those busy sheds when steam was still in full swing. His interest, unbeknown to me, was coincident with mine; but while Shepherd's success as a wildlife artist prevented his further pursuance of railway painting, I was occupied with experiments in technique. Fortuitously for us both, however, we began to look at and paint railways again towards the end of the Sixties.

Some of David Shepherd's 1957 paintings are now in the National Collection at York, but only a few oil sketches remain of the paintings he did at the Nine Elms and Guildford sheds in 1967 due to a disastrous fire at a Durban warehouse where six of those paintings were destroyed after being shown in his exhibition in 1969 at Johannesburg.

It was with great pleasure that my chance came to view all of those paintings in David Shepherd's exhibition at the British Transport Museum in 1968 and I looked in admiration at the flawless Shepherd technique. Interestingly, the link between the artists who were depicting the steam age during the late Sixties and early Seventies, was John Scholes, Curator of Historical Relics at the British Transport Museum; his picture gallery at the museum was the venue for one-man shows for Cuneo, Ellis, Shepherd and myself, and later, Barry Clark.

By the early Seventies, railway artists began to proliferate; some were excellent painters, while others did not know a good composition from a bad one. Among the leading names were artists of such fine calibre as Don Breckon in the West, who turned professional as a result of his magnificent portrayals of the Great Western steam on canvas, and Alan Fearnley in the North, who had been sketching railway subjects in the Sixties but did not paint railways in any volume until he turned professional in 1974. The growing number of railway artists led to the formation of the Guild of Railway Artists, which was confirmation that railway art had established itself – not that it was recognised by the establishment of the art-world who were as prejudiced against us then as they are now.

One wonders if marine art suffered the same prejudice when artists first painted the sea and ships because it is as specialised a field as railway art, yet today it is an accepted art form with the well-established 'Royal Society of Marine Artists' to give it credibility. Time will tell if one day there will be 'Royal Society of Railway Artists'. Perhaps in fifty years' time, railway art will be recognised and the dealers and auction houses of the day will benefit from the work of those railway artists with an established reputation, thus ensuring a healthy financial turnover in this field of art, giving it the respectability that it lacks today.

Both David Shepherd and Don Breckon believe that the possibility of a royal society for railway painters being established is remote. They have met with the same prejudiced attitude to railway art by critics and the London art-world as I have, and Shepherd has also experienced the same prejudice with regard to his wildlife painting. Don Breckon suggests that because critics know nothing of the subject, they are afraid to proclaim the merits of such paintings in case the artist has depicted a technical mistake.

In truth, the critics' blinkered vision is preventing them from taking an expansive look at what is being produced, and the idea that pictures of steam engines, or transport in general, are nothing more than illustrative art is a barrier that perhaps only those excellent artists who are most prominent in the field can with time destroy. Perhaps one day there will be a national collection of transport art with a permanent gallery to house it that would help to give this specialist art-form some credibility. At present, there is no permanent exhibition of railway art and, since the disbanding of the British

'Filtering Light, Pen Green Shed'
oil painting 16in × 12in
Kitson No 48 Criggion simmers gently at the end of the day

(page 47) 'Derbyshire Yeomanry'
oil painting, 30in × 20in
A patriot class and its train exit from Melton Mowbray

Transport Museum, there is no collection of information on the history and development of transport art.

It is always interesting to compare the variety of techniques employed by artists no matter what their subject, but within the railway field, a great many owe a debt of gratitude to Terence Cuneo. I freely admit to the influence he has had on my own style, and it is possible that Fearnley and Breckon would say that they, too, had seriously studied the Cuneo technique. That is not to say, of course, that one artist consciously copies another's techniques or the treatment of certain objects, figures or effects, but a careful study of another artist's work can be adapted, often subconsciously, to become an integral part of one's own style.

I am fascinated not only by my contemporaries' techniques, but by what aspect of the railway scene they have chosen to record or reflect. For example, David Shepherd's interests lie in depicting the run-down engines and grime of the latter years of steam, while Don Breckon looks to the halcyon days of the Great Western Railway at the height of its glory. The latter artist has launched a one-man crusade to re-create the days of the Twenties and Thirties beside the lines of 'God's Wonderful Railway'. His polished and careful technique depicts in the most pleasant of detail everything from the chocolate-and-cream-coloured coaches behind the resplendent engine at their head to the texture of the grasses in the foreground.

Among the watercolourists, Sean Bolan and Peter Annable express in a professional manner their personal view of the railways of yesteryear, and Laurie Hammonds uses his black-and-white techniques to great effect with his graphic studies of life on the railways, the accent of men and machines featuring large within the scope of his vision.

Today, within the railway art movement there is a wide variety of techniques, subject matter and media, although some railway artists are not old enough to remember real steam railways. Just where my own work fits into this pot-pourri of artistic talent is undoubtedly best left to others to judge, but perhaps my catholic taste in the visual arts has led me to look at a wider variety of subjects under the heading of steam than I might otherwise have done, and everything from a line-side allotment hut to the fascinating rhythm of a generating showman's engine at the fairground fill me with the same excitement and desire to paint today as they did forty years ago. Because I painted in the sheds and engine-yards of the Fifties and Sixties, a preference prevails in my work for dirty work-worn engines in grimy, smoky settings as opposed to the bright splendour of railway companies' pre-grouping years.

Terence Cuneo once talked to me about the problem of conveying a sense of weight in art. In essence, it is a matter of tone values, but there is also that indefinable 'something' that comes from within the artist and from an intimate knowledge of the subject, that one could never get from the exclusive use of a photograph. A camera is very useful and forms a part of my sketching equipment, but the photograph should be used only as a reminder of the light or the detail; the fact that the artist has traced every aspect of the subject with enquiring eyes and a pencil is of inestimable value. In an exchange of correspondence with David Shepherd in 1969, we discussed our mutual efforts at painting inside engine-sheds; his comments may be of interest here:

. . . I set up my easel in Crewe, Swindon Works, Cravens, Steel Comp. of Wales (to be showered with sparks and red hot metal chips!), King's Cross station! Unless one has actually done it one can have no idea of the mental, physical torture and exhilaration one can get from doing it in such places. But God, it's worth it – one hour from life is worth a week in the studio.

Such experiences do go into a painting. Cuneo learnt to drive a locomotive well before he ever painted one, so that basic knowledge and understanding became embodied into the feeling he has transmitted onto his canvases.

There comes a point in every painting when the work is complete, although unfortunately the artist does not always recognise it and continues to clutter the result with unnecessary detail or to make those extra touches that ruin a perfectly good piece of lighting. It is so easily done, and in my experience, once the canvas is covered, the artist should constantly watch the whole effect, allowing for some quiet areas where the eye can take a rest; if a painting is so full of busy detail that the eye is made to whirl around the picture, the result will be failure.

Within my own work, I prefer to have sufficient detail around the centres of interest and generally for the detail to subside towards the extremities of the canvas, thus giving some restful areas to contrast or complement the busier areas. Balance is all-important – balance in composition, colour and light. A picture that is overlit will be flat and the result uninspiring; good lighting is for me the most important single factor in any painting.

I am often asked how long a painting has taken to complete. One might as well ask how long is a piece of string. I usually answer glibly 'forty years'. In reality, a watercolour could be on the drawing-board for anything from fifteen minutes to five hours, dependent on the subject – generally, the simpler the subject, the less time the work takes. The same principle applies to oils in that respect, but a railway painting could take anything from a few hours for a very simple subject where little detail or drawing is involved, to two or three weeks for a canvas measuring, for example, 3×4ft, where a great deal of detail is necessary to create engines, background and tracks.

As sometimes happens, an artist will not be able to progress with a piece of work. When this occurs to me, I take the picture off the easel and put it at the end of my studio, sometimes placing it to face the wall, where I will not look at it again for a week or so. Then, when I look at it again, it will be absolutely clear to me what must be done to correct an unsuccessful section or how to progress to finish the work. In assessing the length of time it has taken to produce a painting, one would have to count the hours that the artist's brain was working on the creation, as well as the time he spent working on the canvas.

The average person may have no inkling of the extraordinary amount of effort or the many years of study that have gone into producing a finished painting, even a simple watercolour that may have been completed in a very short time. For example, some of Turner's greatest pictures are among his small and slight watercolours where light rather than location was of the essence. These paintings may have taken only ten minutes to produce, but the artist's genius shines out from them indisputably.

The Norfolk-born landscape painter Edward Seago also produced fresh watercolours with speed with stunning results. His energetic and bold approach with oils has been an inspiration to me since I first encountered his work during the Fifties. Sadly, he produced to my knowledge only one railway painting, but had he painted steam, his broad, direct technique would have surely resulted in some superb works of art.

Turner, Cuneo, Shepherd and Seago, together with some lesser known artists, have undoubtedly influenced my own approach and style. A 'Weston', for example, is easily distinguishable from a work by any of those other artists. How easily those influences can be detected in my work is difficult for me to judge, but others may be able to see the influences with a detached and more distant perspective.

Undoubtedly, painting steam engines is a difficult occupation, for whereas with landscape painting the artist can bend a tree or move a whole plantation if he wishes, the details of a steam locomotive and its environs cannot be changed and there are many knowledgeable critics only too anxious to point out any faults.

Many years ago, I was working on a painting of a Black 5 ascending Beatock summit. The smoke was belching out of the chimney and the engine was obviously straining to make the ascent. The painting was on my easel in my small studio in Leicester, when a man from the Electricity Board came to read the meter. Having done so, he viewed the almost completed painting and asked why the engine was working so hard with empty coaches. In my ignorance, I asked him why he thought the coaches were empty, because I would hardly paint people in at the angle depicted. 'Well,' he replied, 'It's your head code, you see, that's the code for empty stock; I know, because I used to drive them.' I then learned that I should double-check even the smallest facts, especially when I was working from a photograph that was being used only as a basis for the actual composition. Such attention to detail is essential, no matter what the subject of a work of art.

Terence Cuneo explained to me how one week he might be a construction engineer and another a beagler. Few artists enjoy such variety, but in Cuneo's case, he keeps two easels in his studio and often changes from one canvas to the other. Cuneo maintains that the change keeps him fresh and alert, thus preventing him from becoming tired with a painting. My own preference is to work on one painting at a time, in short bursts of an hour or two with small breaks between to assist the subconscious mind to do its work and to keep the inspiration flowing, until the work is complete.

The almost completed picture of the beagle hunt was on Cuneo's easel when I visited him in 1980; the dogs and the figures in their blue jackets were in a group facing to the front, but each figure had a completely blank face. I asked if he had drawn each head or perhaps even photographed them. 'Oh heavens, no,' he said. 'They're all coming here individually to have their faces painted in, all, that is, except that poor devil,' he jabbed a finger at one unfortunate. 'He's kicked the blessed bucket.'

With me that day was the Hon. John Gretton, now Lord Gretton, a fellow railway enthusiast who was once joint-owner of the Great Western locomotive *Pendennis Castle* and had a wonderful miniature passenger-carrying line around the family estate at Stapleford Hall in Leicestershire. John had asked me to introduce him to Cuneo so that he could add one of Terence's railway paintings to his collection.

We were shown a number of large paintings and one that captivated me was an ageing and dirty Class 50 at Soltau shed in West Germany called *The Sole Survivor*, but the one that caught John's eye and which he ultimately bought was a huge canvas entitled 'Monarchs of Steam'. The painting was the result of some days the artist had spent in the yards at Boulogne sketching the last of those gargantuan giants of the Nord.

Cuneo's studio is full of reminders of his travels worldwide. It is spacious with elegant windows that look out onto a small lawn, and was formerly a beamed and raftered barn. I was very impressed with that room on my first visit and have probably subconsciously modelled my own studio, converted from a stable block, along similar lines.

Artists' studios vary enormously according to personal preferences or the limitations of expenditure. For some artists, a back bedroom is all that is required, for others a shed in the garden, or an attic, bare and paint bespattered, is thought to be the ideal solution for the right creative atmosphere. My priority is to have plenty of space, not only for painting but to house books, models and antiques – the latter a hobby I pursue with enthusiasm. My easel where oil paintings are produced is situated in the main room of the studio. There is an entrance section and a room for displaying pictures and where I often write. The watercolour tables are in a light and airy extension to the main room which overlooks the lawn and garden. Across the lawn is a separate picture gallery which is opened only for special events or by appointment. The tranquillity of this gallery helps me to keep calm in my day-to-day proceedings and in the all-important business of fostering creative inspiration. Too many interruptions can play havoc with the flow of one's thought processes, and there is nothing more annoying than disjointed flashes of action on a painting, as became apparent in my earlier years when my studio was open to the public.

The right studio is therefore very important, no matter whether it is humble or grand, because a masterpiece cannot be produced if an artist is half-hearted and working in bad conditions with the wrong equipment.

At the end of a year, an artist should review his work and select one or two pictures that he considers to be above average. Such drastic selection should help an artist to improve on his abilities. An artist strives constantly to improve his standard of work, but the truly inspired works of art, the ones that an artist will look back on in years to come with a small glow of self-satisfaction, are indeed few and far between.

5 ENGINES IN INDUSTRY

The long grass waved gently in a summer breeze brushing against the rusting wheels of a long-silent locomotive, the faded apple-green of the once-smart livery flaking and blackened with oil and rust. It was the Sixties and there was an air of abandon about the old Black Hawthorne locomotive. As I stood aboard the foot-plate, my mind went back over some twenty years to a time when the quarries at Desborough in the heart of Northamptonshire's iron-stone country were a frequent haunt of mine.

There was little doubt in my mind that as a youngster I had watched this same locomotive, bright and shining, at work in the quarries at Desborough in company with others of a similar vintage.

The various quarry systems at Desborough linked up with the Midland main line near Desborough and Rothwell Station, and I could hardly wait on getting off the train there on those childhood visits to climb over the stile by the road-bridge and run through the fields, chest-high with summer corn, towards the quarries, and in particular to 'shaky bridge'. This was a spectacular wooden structure that carried the foot-path across the width of the quarry. The one-plank foot-walk bounced unnervingly up and down in a hair-raising fashion and was supported high above the quarry floor on slender wooden piers. As a boy, it was exciting both for its pronounced wobbly bounce and because the locomotives with their wagon-loads of ore passed directly underneath, and it was fun to try to drop pebbles down the chimneys.

The engines were 0-4-0 and 0-6-0 saddle tanks, most of them built by Hudswell Clarke of Leeds and one built in 1895 was on track-lifting work at the close of the quarry in 1966, she looked weather-worn and battle-scarred – a far cry from those bright green, shining engines of yesteryear, with their red connecting-rods and polished brass-plates on their cab sides.

Such was my introduction to industrial steam, so different from the massive and powerful engines of the main lines. Of course, as a boy I knew nothing of their work or of the extent of the iron-stone lines that ran throughout Northamptonshire, Rutland and East Leicestershire. It was possible to see the engines at Desborough only from my viewpoint on 'shaky bridge' and I regarded them almost as toy trains.

In later years, I learnt that many such quarries were formed after the building of the Midland main line south of Leicester when, as a result, huge deposits of iron-ore were discovered. These pits developed alongside the line between Market Harborough and Wellingborough and by 1880 about thirty pits were producing an output of over a million tons of ore a year.

Wellingborough itself became known as Iron Town and, prior to the turn of the century, boasted as many as seventeen blast furnaces. Kettering, too, had its furnaces and both locations had their own narrow-gauge railway systems. It was a delight to see the locomotives at Kettering furnaces and I thought they were so quaint that they would have done credit to Roland Emnett himself. This 3ft-gauge line had half a dozen engines of such great character that they were irresistible as subjects for the brush. There were three Manning Wardle 0-6-0 saddle tanks and three delightful Black Hawthornes, one of which, *Kettering Furnaces No 2*, was the subject of a close-up watercolour done in the early 1960s shortly before both the furnaces and the line finally disappeared in 1963.

I now regret that Kettering did not receive more of my attention, for although the system and furnaces were small by comparison with their near-neighbours at Wellingborough and Corby, there was from an artist's viewpoint so much of interest and character that in retrospect I regard it as the epitome of the blast-furnace/iron-ore industry scene.

Narrow-gauge railways hold a fascination of their own; the diminutive size of the engines and invariably their great age add much to their quaintness and character. The tramway between the quarry and the furnaces at Kettering retained much of its Victorian origins in both atmosphere and hardware. Built before the development of road transport, such small systems as those at Kettering and Wellingborough where no actual meeting with the standard gauge was needed, were the cheapest form of tramway to build. The narrow and light track was better able to follow the contours of the land, and sharper curves were much easier for both engines and rolling stock to negotiate.

Another factor in favour of the narrow gauge was its facility to be moved easily for either realignments of the track or complete resiting to allow for changes in operating conditions – an important requirement in the iron-ore pits where operations had to keep up with the advancement of the working face.

Throughout the Midlands' iron fields, most pits worked with standard-gauge lines from as far afield as Oxfordshire in the south of the area to Lincolnshire in the north-east, and these little railway systems ran across the entire iron-stone region, giving joy to both artists and railway enthusiasts alike.

The mineral companies and steelworks that owned the quarries had bought a great variety of ancient locomotives from a diversity of private builders and so, within any area of a few square miles, it was possible to see an enormous selection of these old-timers hard at work.

In time, many of the private iron-stone companies became a part of the giant iron and steel works, some companies disappearing totally in the process. It was as a result of the decline in demand for home-produced ore (that from Australia and Sweden being a better financial proposition), that caused the closure of so many of the mineral workings in the region. From over a million tons a week between 1869 and 1872, the entire output had fallen just a century later to a mere three thousand tons. Ironically, the drop in demand for home-produced ore was due to the very high rate of freight charges on our railways and this, combined with the better iron content of the Swedish ore, signalled the end for many pits. Improved shipping, the expansion and rationalisation of the steel works nearer the coast, all contributed to the run-down of the Midland ore-fields and furnaces, so, with the demise of the Wellingborough and Kettering works, only the great stronghold of Corby itself remained to enter the 1970s.

During the late Sixties I began to realise that these systems were fast disappearing and this realisation, together with my regrets at not painting and drawing more of the Kettering works, caused me to write to the Stewart's and Lloyd's Company for permission to paint whenever it was possible in both their steel-works and minerals section of the Corby area.

To my surprise, I was welcomed wholeheartedly in both divisions and in retrospect it is satisfying to look back at the results of the time and effort I put into the project. It was not easy, however, for me to get from my home just outside Leicester to Corby because I was still a struggling amateur painter, and had either to raise the bus fare or thumb a lift. I was given a pass which enabled me to wander at will anywhere at any time, and once I had reported my presence I was free to do whatever I pleased.

The great steelworks of Corby represented to me almost a century of progress, development and decline, for it was in the 1870s that huge deposits of iron-ore were discovered in the area immediate to Corby as a result of the excavations of the Midland Railway, and in 1880 that Samuel Lloyd of Lloyd & Lloyd, the Birmingham tube-makers, visited the site which led to his forming the Cardigan Iron Ore Company. The mineral rights were leased from the landowner, Lord Cardigan. By the turn of the century, three separate quarries were being worked, each having its own standard-gauge railway system with connections to the Midland Railway's line from Kettering to Manton. By 1910, two blast furnaces had been built alongside the quarries and consequently the first Corby-made iron was in production.

It was soon found necessary to build a stud of locomotives to work within the complex of the furnaces and in 1911 two 0-6-0 saddle-tank locomotives arrived from Andrew Barclay's named *Ironworks 1 and 2* and a third engine from Hudswell Clarke in 1919. One of the original Andrew Barclay engines had only just finished work during my visits in the Sixties.

The standard livery for all the steelworks engines was yellow – this had been adopted following the separation of the minerals and steel divisions in 1950. Obviously, it made the engines all the more visible among the dark and dangerous structures at the heart of the furnaces. The engines that were used in the furnaces were mainly outside cylinder types, unlike the quarry stud, but within the works the danger was of debris falling onto the tracks which could easily damage the inside cylinder types. Hawthorne Leslie 0-6-0 saddle tanks alongside the larger Hunslet 50550 class saddle tanks comprised the majority of the engine stud and most were well-battered work-horses in contrast to the attractive appearance of those in the Pen Green engine-shed of the minerals section.

The work of the steelworks locomotives included the moving of slag from the furnaces to the asphalt plant and feeding coal into the huge coke ovens. The locomotives might also be seen hauling loads of completed tubes from the works to the exchange sidings with the main line. Similarly, they were employed to bring in raw materials, such as coal, slack and limestone which were all needed for the steel-making process, from the BR sidings. From across the tracks there was a magnificent view of these operations, with the dramatic backdrop of the mighty furnaces in full spate.

One of the sights I often watched with fascination were the train loads of molten iron being trundled from the blast furnaces to the steel plant, and I

Robert Stephenson and Hawthorne locomotive No 53 shown in a water-colour (22in × 15in) done at Pen Green in the late Sixties. The Hudswell Clarke 'Rhos' is in the background

recall watching this operation one afternoon from a bridge above the tracks.

The huge cauldrons of red-hot iron glowing with yellows and fluorescent oranges glinted in the sunlight. At the same time, while the sun was still out, a sudden shower drenched the scene and caused a dramatic rainbow effect to hang over the cauldrons immediately below me. It was a scene of incredible incandescent beauty; droplets of water, pure silver and gold, glistened in the sunlight, and the fine rainbow-coloured spray over the cauldron wagons was so translucent and ethereal that it was doubtful whether it could ever be painted. It was a spell-binding moment and a sight that remains clear in my memory to this day.

That such beauty exists in these dirty industrial surroundings is indisputable, but one wonders how much those who work there actually see for themselves, for while I stood at that scene feeling overwhelmed at the vision that so entranced me, others went about their duties oblivious to the splendour that in the space of no more than two or three minutes was nothing short of mircaculous.

From the steelworks it was a short trip to the quarries' engine-shed at Pen Green. The shed's interior was large by any standards and it boasted no less than eight roads. For the most part it was well lit from above, although there was the odd gloomy corner where an engine might lurk in a half-light.

I captured one of the older engines, a Hudswell Clarke of 1918, in such conditions and sat down to produce a watercolour of old *Rhos*, cold and silent at the end of her working life. It was one of many paintings that I produced within that shed, the engines in their rich deep-green livery with red connecting-rods making attractive subject matter.

The Kitsons and Manning Wardles were my particular favourites. There were also a number of locomotives built by Robert Stephenson and Hawthorne, and it puzzled me that all three designs looked similar, until I discovered that Manning Wardle had been taken over by Kitson's in 1927. In turn, Robert Stephenson and Hawthorne's took over the good-will of Kitson's, so the same basic design had been handed on and remained almost unaltered for about sixty years, a great credit to the original Manning Wardle design.

In 1950, a fleet of seven very large 0-6-0 saddle tanks were also purchased from Robert Stephenson and Hawthorne and these were still very much in evidence, but although they added variety to the stud, I seldom felt inclined to draw them at close quarters. They were similar in appearance to the Hunslet Austerity saddle-tank engines in common use nationally, but as far as picture-making was concerned, I tended to depict them at a distance working in the quarries, although they had, in fact, been purchased originally for work on the Cowthick and Harringworth extensions.

The smaller Manning Wardle locomotives were more commonly seen at work in the complex of quarries that surrounded the loco shed, water-tower and workshops of the Pen Green depot. Permanent way and equipment trains were always in evidence because of the constant amount of track-work that was necessary to follow the course of the various diggers at work in the pits.

In the quarries, tranquillity and activity lived side by side, especially in the heat of a summer's day. The rich red earth of the Northamptonshire countryside, the hedgerows alive with wildlife, the rustle of leaves in a wooded spinney or the lyrical warbling of a lark hovering high above, were all a part of the setting of the iron-ore industry, in acute contrast to the workings that took place in the deep gashes below the plateau of the natural landscape. The sharp sound of a loaded mineral train, the engine barking its exhaust skywards, and the clattering of the wagons echoed dramatically across the landscape as the little train, fully loaded with ore, extricated itself from the quarry and across the fields towards the distant glow of the ever-hungry furnaces.

Memories of the sounds of these engines at work linger on, especially those of still winter days when the clarity of sound was such that one could hear distant echoes across the countryside from other pits, and it was possible to guess by the sound which particular engine was working there and thereby repeatedly acknowledge the individuality of the steam locomotive.

There were so many exciting and visually stimulating operations within the quarries and the steel complex at Corby that if one never left the track-side, there was enough to paint for years to come. The decline in the industry had, however, taken a hold, for by 1970 only six of the twenty-five engines that the Pen Green locomotive stud had housed in 1960 were in regular daily service. Quarries began to close and the amount of ore being despatched away from Corby for use elsewhere was reduced to a very disappointing level.

The days when the night sky glowed to a fiery red and the urgent sounds of the on-going circle of furnace activity blended with that of the iron-ore railways have subsided to a mere shadow of their former dramatic glory, and now, of course, steam on the railway system has been completely eclipsed.

The sights and the sounds of the iron-ore industry have largely disappeared from the Midlands, and all those busy pits with their individual steam railway systems no longer exist; indeed, one can search the whole region today to try to find traces of the previous widespread activity and fail to do so. The land has been reclaimed and given over once again to agriculture; where huge pits existed, now lie fields of crops and plantations of spruce and larch. The skylark sings still over the Northamptonshire countryside, but the echoes of the engines can now exist only in the memory and imagination.

Greater than the large number of engines working in the iron-ore complexes were the numerous locomotives in use in the coal-mining industry. Smaller, private companies in all areas of industry employed anything from a single engine to a stud of a dozen or more.

One company with only a single engine was the granite-quarrying firm at Mountsorrel in Leicestershire. The urge to revisit the little one-lane shed to paint would often see me cycling the ten miles or so on a Saturday or Sunday when the works were totally deserted and I could have the shed entirely to myself. I never asked for permission to enter because the shed was open on

'Day's Work Done'
oil painting, 16in × 12in

all sides and my right to be there was never challenged, despite the fact that the place was hazardous for the foolhardy and over-inquisitive.

One day I decided to paint on the top edge of the quarry looking down onto the crushing plant and its attendant machinery. It was a windy day with a threat of heavy rain, and I was forced to tie down my easel with some rope to some bricks on the ground. The painting under production was a thickly painted oil that rattled on the easel in the gusty conditions. The painting was almost complete when the rain came down so suddenly, accompanied by such fierce gusts of wind that the easel together with the canvas blew away over the edge of the quarry.

I tried to catch them, but in the process totally lost my balance, falling some twenty feet onto a wet conveyor belt that was used for carrying rock down into the crushing plant. The painting, my easel, some brushes and the palette, preceded my own progress on the downward scramble; neither myself nor my possessions had managed to get a grip on the wet rubber surface of the conveyor. My painting fell over the edge about half-way down, but the easel and I continued at a frightening pace towards the gaping hole of the crusher; once inside, it would have been impossible to have escaped, even if I had survived the fall. Flinging my legs wide, I miraculously bridged the two posts on either side of the entrance hole. The easel was lost forever, crushed to dust no doubt when the works were switched on again.

Having escaped that fate, I shook uncontrollably as I began the climb back to the top of the quarry. I retrieved my painting en route, but it was severely damaged by smudged paint and granite dust. I then learnt to have a greater respect for the dangers inherent on any industrial site – a lesson I shall never forget.

The engine-shed was less dangerous and had some interesting subject matter to paint. Long, narrow and low-lit, its thick stone walls were sometimes illuminated by patches of sunlight that streamed through the broken iron-framed window-panes. Ivy, too, crept in to soften the harshness of the stonework. Whenever *Elizabeth* was in steam, the smells and simmering gurgles could be savoured; smoke from her chimney always hung in the air and drifted idly towards the smoke vents above; hot oil would dribble down the wheel cranks, and little streams of shattered hot-water bubbles would trickle down the oily metal to splash into the puddles on the floor.

It was good to feel the warmth of the engine in that dank interior and I was always disappointed whenever I arrived to find the engine cold – which unfortunately was more often than not. *Elizabeth* was, and still is, an 0-4-0 saddle-tank locomotive built by Peckett's. Her only companion in the shed was a small diesel shunter named *The Chairman*. Now preserved at the Rutland Railway Museum, *Elizabeth* was in her latter days at Mountsorrel in poor condition, her faded apple-green livery dull with patches of rust, hand-rails bent, maker's plates missing and leaking at every joint.

'Ironstone Line'
oil painting, 14in × 10in
Oakley quarry, Corby

'Elizabeth at Mountsorrel'
(22in × 15in) The old Peckett saddle tank in her ramshackle shed at Mountsorrel quarry in Leicestershire. From a watercolour painted on the spot in the Sixties

For me, however, these defects were no drawback – there was a special magic inside that shed, whatever the weather or the light or the fact that *Elizabeth* was no more than an ordinary, battered old engine, and despite the fact that the wind could howl through the length of the place like a wind-tunnel.

On such cold, windy days there was only one place to retreat and that was to a small room leading off the shed about half-way down. It was the rest-room for the workmen and it offered warmth from a lovely old cast-iron range. It was a godsend in winter when frozen fingers were brought back to life, and the enormous black kettle was forever on the hob for a welcome cup of tea.

Another small engine-shed in Leicestershire was well worth a visit to see the engines and the qualities of the shed from an artistic viewpoint. That, too, was never locked and my Sunday visits when the shed was unmanned, were also secretive. As at Mountsorrel, I was fascinated by the ramshackle nature of the shed; slates missing off the roof exposed the rafters in places to the sky above; broken, draughty windows looked towards the end section with its clutter of fitters' benches, tools and equipment; and the encroaching ivy crept in through every nook and cranny, threatening to take over the work-benches.

In 1958 on one of my Sunday visits, I was enthralled to find one of the 0-4-0

Hunslet saddle-tank engines stripped down in this cramped section of the old shed. It was a superb subject for a painting and consequently I produced a very large watercolour of the scene, although it was not a successful painting. My technique in those early years was not sufficiently developed to deal with such difficult subject matter: the dim light of the interior, the filtration of light through the broken windows and the way it fell across the rusting locomotive, coupled with the amount of drawing that was necessary to depict the clutter of the surroundings was at the time more than a relative beginner could cope with successfully. However, in retrospect I am glad that at least an attempt was made, for the sketch and painting still exist in my archives ready for future and more confident attempts at the subject.

There were three Hunslet locomotives at Groby in those days – Nos 1, 2 and 5. Records show that No 2 was stripped down in 1958 and it seems certain that this was the engine I painted. The records also show that a third Hunslet, Groby Granite No 5 of 1901, was cut up at the quarry in 1961.

From my many visits to Groby, I remember in particular the two large oil paintings I produced inside the shed of the two Hunslet saddle tanks in their dark green livery: that marvellous day when the watercolour of No 2 under repair was produced, and a final visit there some time after 1966 when the engines had been scrapped and the shed lay derelict and open to the sky. It was a day of brilliant sunlight and the result of that visit is a small oil painting recently completed from an earlier watercolour entitled 'Dazzling Light, Groby'. It is a sad subject but one that is full of colour and atmosphere, symbolic of the decline nationwide of industrial steam.

The variety of settings for industrial engines knew no bounds and the choice was endless if one considered the more well-known locations where fleets of engines could be observed at their various duties. Apart from the iron-ore, steel and coal industries, the china-clay industry boasted a number of engines, as did Bowater's paper-works in Kent; there were the Welsh-slate workings where beautiful little brass-domed engines clung to the mountainside ledges to carry the slate from high in the clouds, and in contrast, the Seaham harbour-dock lines and the Pallion shipyard complex in the North-East where the intriguing little fleet of crane engines performed their various tasks to perfection.

The gas and power stations had steam engines, and contractors used them during the nineteenth century to build the main lines of the railway networks.

Cadbury's used steam at their Bournville works; Bass, Ratcliffe and Gretton had an extensive system serving their breweries; and the chalk pits of Kent and the limestone working of Derbyshire also used steam propulsion.

Where the British coal industry is concerned, my own attention and inspiration have found expression in the dramatic valleys of the South Wales coalfields. It was during my first visit to South Wales that I became attracted to the landscape of the valleys and more particularly to the dramatic and emotive imagery of the mines and the railway systems that served them.

To me, the valleys of South Wales had everything for the painter: the opportunity to create in a natural landscape surrounded by the enclosing hillsides, the mine workings with their dramatic build-up to the pit-head gear, and the engines that trundled back and forth with their loads of jet-black coal creating steam and smoke in an already evocative and atmospheric landscape that had its origins deep rooted in the years of the Industrial Revolution.

From the Fifties through to the Seventies, I witnessed the slow decline of the South Wales coalfields, a decline that has become so advanced as to be in danger of approaching oblivion. Many of the collieries have now disappeared, leaving behind silent memories of men and machines and often whole communities. The rusting pit-head gear often now stands desolate like some iron sentinel reflecting the lives and deaths of those who had toiled beneath its gaunt and lonely framework.

Ex-Great Western pannier tank locomotive at Tyseley (pencil sketch)

It is impossible to separate the Welsh mines from the people. The coal for which they toiled deep in the bowels of the earth beneath their dark, Satanic mines was exported around the world, making the valleys the very hub of the age of steam. In the demise of the Welsh coal-mining industry lie the dreams of men, both rich and poor, of engineers a century and a half ago whose skills made way for prosperity and progress, of those whose labours saw them entombed by disaster, and those young hearts at the village of Aberfan whose lives were denied by the shifting of the very earth for which their forefathers had toiled to secure their future.

In some valleys, all trace of the pit and the lives of those for whom it was everything have now been returned to nature, grassed over in an attempt to make it look as though nothing more had ever happened there save the grazing of the sheep. But lift the carpet of the grass a little, and one will see the dust and ashes of a previous existence whose ghosts cry out in desperation over the futility of the demise of their industry and with it their way of life; and for those who have remained to see another day, the constant ignominy of unemployment and hardship is an unhappy fact of everyday existence.

Is it wrong, one wonders, for an artist to reflect on such things while painting the mines and valleys of these people? I cannot think so, for although the composition of the picture will be the same irrespective of the historical background, its inspiration is based as much on the feelings conveyed – the sadness, the pathos and compassion – as on the weather, light and atmosphere.

Recently, I drove from Pontypool and ascended the deeply wooded valley that looks down on Hafodyrynys colliery along the road that rises to pass beside the pit and its gaunt concrete structures. Looking through the fir trees into the steep narrow gorge, I saw a scene where little moved, the buildings were silent, the tracks were rusting and not an engine was to be seen.

Hafodyrynys was different from other pits, its location in an alpine-like, thickly wooded valley, and its modern rectangular concrete buildings formed a series of overbridges at the heart of the mine through which the steam engines trundled as their whistles bounced an eerie echo up the length of the valley. It was a joy to paint, an evocative place where the engines were dwarfed by the buildings and the sheer height of the enclosing hillsides.

The valleys of South Wales are threaded by the railway. At every valley bottom, the convergence of lines links the communities together, one valley to another, by a weaving metallic thread, the railway being always prominent at every twist of the landscape. In the steam years, the railway was well used, carrying passengers the length and breadth of the complex system of routes throughout the valleys. Often the trains on these routes comprised no more than two or three coaches which were usually drawn by a Great Western pannier tank locomotive.

'North Rhondda Platform'
oil painting, 14in × 10in
A miner's special at Glyncorrwg pit in the Corrwg valley (Jessop Collection)

Oakdale Colliery, South Wales. A scene typical of the dramatic build-up of buildings to the pit-head gear itself – an ink sketch done in the early Seventies

These engines became so much a part of the landscape that in later years they infiltrated into the mines alongside the Hunslets and the Pecketts. They were often used on the workmen's trains which took the miners to the pits and special platforms, such as the North Rhondda platform just a hundred yards or so from the Glyncorrwg South pit on the Corrwg valley line, were built to accommodate this facility. There was something special about these miners' trains as they clickety-clicked along the valley and those with the old-fashioned clerestory-roofed carriages, old and somewhat woebegone, had a character all of their own. The locomotive always pushed its train up the line, the leading coach being fitted with observation windows and a warning bell.

The Corrwg valley line was opened in 1863, but from 1908 it was worked by the Port Talbot Railway by agreement with the GWR. From 1918 to 1930 a public passenger service was in operation, but after that date unadvertised miners' trains continued to be run because there was no road access to the North Rhondda pit at the top end of the valley. When this pit closed in 1963, the spectacle of the miners' train rapidly became a thing of the past, the last service between South pit halt and Glyncorrwg being withdrawn in November 1964. Thus, another unique piece of the railway history of the region was lost with the closure of the mines.

As the pits disappeared one by one, it became a personal quest to see as much of them as was possible on my somewhat infrequent visits to South Wales. Merthyr Vale, Blaenavon, Abercynon, Oakdale, Celynen and Britannia, all became subjects for my sketchbook and canvases, and then there was Mountain Ash, that most atmospheric of settings, where the skeletonic winding gear overlooked the gentle sweep of the railway tracks with their endless rows of waiting wagons.

The Mountain Ash system was built to accommodate several pits in the vicinity including Abercynon, Deep Duffryn, Penrhiwceiber and Aberaman, which were all set in the Cynon valley. Besides the pits hereabouts, the railway also served a gas-works, a granary and, of course, the forbidding furnacite plant at Abercwmboi. It was the transportation of coal-dust waste to this plant from Penrhiwceiber colliery that played a large part in this system becoming one of the last strongholds of steam in the Welsh coalfields, with four locomotives working at the close of the Seventies.

At Merthyr Vale the composition of the pit-head gear made a strong background for the engines that were still in service – only just at times, for they were not in the best of running order. An 0-6-0 saddle tank (No 6) and a ramshackle Barclay side tank were assisted by an ex-GWR pannier that was rattling itself to pieces as it pitched and rolled its leaking progress over the

'Black and Gold at Merthyr'
oil painting, 12in × 10in

roller-coaster tracks each time it heaved its heavy loads of coal out of the pit yards.

The engines here were no different from those in any other colliery as far as condition was concerned, and it was a great tribute to the mechanics whose job it was to keep them running that, despite the lack of spares and the draughty, cramped and very difficult working conditions of the leaking sheds in which they operated, somehow these men managed repeatedly to inject a life-blood of steam back into an engine that most would have considered lost, short of a total rebuild.

The engines of the coalfields of the Sixties and Seventies were always battered, rusting and invariably blackened by the dust of the earth below their tracks. They were a special breed, like the men who drove and maintained them, and if ever proof were needed to substantiate the affinity between man and machine, one need look no further than the lines of the Welsh pits and their desolate little fitters' shops.

The last time my journeyings took me to Merthyr Vale, I sat by the tracks and thought again about the terrible disaster at Aberfan just down the road, and the awful price these people have paid for their way of life, the scant reward bestowed upon them in recent years and the hopelessness of the redundant miner who knew nothing else other than the pit. Where should he go now to apply his skills to cull from the earth the black gold that once so readily filled the lines of rusting wagons?

This thought inspired me to do a small painting of the pit-head gear at Merthyr Vale, with a view into a low golden sun. It was to be a picture full of light that I hoped would epitomise much of what I felt about the pits. The silhouetted winding gear is black against the light, and old No 6 creaks and wheezes with steam leaking from every joint, while the smoke from her chimney drifts across the light that is reflected into the pools of water between the glinting rails.

The title 'Black and Gold, Merthyr' seems appropriate for this very small painting that reflects, perhaps more than any other, my personal vision of the mines and their railways at the end of a once magnificent era in the chapters of our industrial history.

To conclude my thoughts and memories of industrial steam, I will return to the place where those recollections began, within the iron-ore and steel-making industry, but this time to the small ironworks that once stood proudly at the top of Asfordby Hill in Leicestershire's attractive landscape.

Holwell ironworks was small compared with the vast sprawl of the Corby works. As a schoolboy, it was easy to cycle out to this most fascinating of places. The visual attractions of the old Bessemer furnaces drew me to attempt many a scribble within its fiery heart, and to watch with rapture the comings and goings of the little engines that fussed about between the towering cylinders of the furnace.

Then, some twenty years later and long after the furnaces had gone, one could look across the rolling landscape of the Wreake valley to Asfordby Hill where, from a distance, there was no longer even the remotest sign of an iron-making plant. I went again to what was left of the old works because it was apparent that steam was still just alive in 1969, although the nature of the industry surrounding the tracks had changed from what it had been in the old blast-furnace days. Sure enough, there was Holwell No 18, built by Andrew Barclay in 1923, looking resplendent in a bright green livery, complementing the clean red of her connecting rods and wasp-striped buffer beam. She looked hale and hearty and ready for action.

Although it was pleasing to see No 18 in steam and looking so spruce, my attention was increasingly drawn to a couple of old saddle tanks that had been dumped, quite literally, on the scrap heap. They looked so sad as they awaited their fate at the hands of the cutter's torch, that I had no option but to draw them. Several angles made outstanding compositions, and the pathos that was inherent in the engines' position amid piles of scrap metal and an old ladle from the furnace, spoke volumes about the decline of the steel and coal industries and the cessation of steam in general. The scene inspired me to produce three drawings that day and to do an oil sketch, a procedure watched by an audience of men from the plant who seemingly had little else to do.

It has been one of those glorious November days that started with a silvery mist that slowly cleared as the sun shone through. By the early evening, the lowering sun was turning the rusts and ochres of the two old engines to brilliant oranges, and the golden glow from the sky reflected its glory to glint in highlights of pure gold atop of the engines. The steam age had become eclipsed, and all that could be said about it lay before one's eyes in the combination of light and emotive imagery.

Such days spent outside sketching and painting can never be forgotten because they are so satisfying and rewarding, regardless of the quality of one's work. From those several sketches done at Holwell that day in 1969, several oils have been produced over the years, all of which now hang on other people's walls. Recently, I produced another oil of the early evening light and the two old engines from that time, and this hangs on my own wall and will remain there as a reminder of a lovely day's sketching and, perhaps more importantly, as a poignant statement about all that has gone in the turn-around of so many empires.

Stanton No 27 at Holwell Works (pencil rough)

(page 64) 'Goliaths of the Night'
oil painting
A Fowler showman's engine provides the light and power as it gently rocks back and forth on its chocks, a glittering array of bright lights and burnished brass

(page 65) 'Requiem for Steam'
oil painting, 16in × 12in
*The end of the line at Holwell Works (*Jessop Collection*)*

Stanton NO 27

6 RAILWAY TERRITORY

Childhood visits to Northamptonshire relatives always meant a journey on the train from Leicester – an event of great excitement to a ten-year-old boy with a fascination for all that the journey entailed and it would be a highlight to be recalled for weeks afterwards. The journey in 1945 would take us to Desborough and Rothwell, a well-kept, iron-stone built station on the main Leicester to London line, just south of Market Harborough, on the metals of the LMS railway.

Once at Desborough, however, the desire to stay for long in my aunt's house in Union Street soon dissipated and I was soon back at the station to watch the trains rushing through. Somehow, there was never enough time to be off on my own, so it was prudent to divide my time between the delights of the 'toy trains' below shaky bridge in the quarry and the station where the frightening roar of the expresses shook the very foundations of the platform and made the gas-lamps chatter in chorus down the length of the station.

Once again, as I sat by the booking-office wall as far away from the

The Crossing Cottage, Beverley, East Yorkshire (pencil drawing)

platform edge as possible, I felt as overawed at the sheer size and power of the expresses as I had some two years earlier with my fiery dragon, except that now they had come to be recognised as mickeys or Jubilees, tankers and compounds.

Desborough greatly influenced my childhood, for it was not only here that my enthusiasm for industrial steam began, but I also became intrigued with the gentle comings and goings of the country station. There appeared to be no rush in such places, no rules, no dos and don'ts, nobody seemed to care if a small boy wanted to sit on a seat to watch the trains go by and observe the porter tending the flower-beds or painting the edging stones around his pretty little gardens with crisp white paint. It didn't matter, and as a consequence I fell in love with the atmosphere of these quiet rural oases where life seemed so relaxed and where the only disruption of the tranquillity lay in the dramatic build-up of an approaching express – there was no official loud-speaker announcement to stand clear, of course, but if someone happened to remember, he might shout an inaudible warning.

The same person would also appear with unfailing regularity when a local

Crossing Cottage

train stopped at the station. Then he could be heard above the slam of the doors and the contented hiss of escaping steam to shout 'Daresbro and Roal, Daresbro, Daresbro and Roal' as he walked the length of the platform.

It was still a time when the enamel advertising signs added colour to the surroundings and Stephens' inks and Sunlight soap or Craven 'A' would peep out from between the hollyhocks and the lupins of the flower-beds to try to persuade us to write more, or wash more, or smoke ourselves into an early grave. Colour and smartness abounded, the rich brown-gold of the Northamptonshire iron-stone setting off the flowers and the white painted fences to perfection.

When we returned to the station at night for our homeward journey, the place had taken on a totally different atmosphere. From the dim yellow light of the hanging gas-lamps, long strange shadows slowly swung to and fro, imbuing the place with an eery and unreal atmosphere, the cool night air crisp as we automatically gravitated towards the red light on the signal at the platform end.

The scent from the flowers on a summer's evening at the further end would suddenly become lost in the excitement of the approach of our homeward train. The belated clanging of a bell half-way up the platform made us automatically step back to watch the massive black silhouette silently glide towards us at what seemed like an enormous speed. Surely it could never stop, but as the colossal bulk of the engine flew past so that we caught a phrenetic glimpse of a bright orange glow of fire and reflected lights on steam-wreathed levers and dials, the two men silhouetted against the firelight appeared to be doing nothing at all on that foot-plate to halt the flight of the machine.

With what always seemed like amazing rapidity, the train did stop and suddenly we were aboard to the accompanying slam of doors, a shrill whistle, a few shouts, and 'Daresbro and Roal' faded rapidly into the distance.

Desborough, of course, was rural enough in those days but it was not a true country branch station due to its siting on the main line from St Pancras to the North. My discovery of the even more sleepy delights of the truly rural branch-line station came some years later. One line drifted out into the wilds of the rolling East Leicestershire countryside to the beautiful Vale of Belvoir and could eventually land the unsuspecting passenger in either Grantham (if an exchange was necessary for a proper train), or Skegness, Mablethorpe or even Hunstanton, if dipping a toe in the sea was a suitable alternative.

The journey started from beneath the huge canopy of Belgrave Road Station in Leicester, a piece of Great Northern architecture so substantial with its echoes of St Pancras, that one cannot imagine that it was ever justified by the number of passengers who departed from beneath its imposing portals, even in the heady days of the pre-grouping railway companies. By the Fifties, activity was spasmodic and for most of the time the station was deserted. Maybe a Skegness special would be waiting to depart with a woebegone B1 at its head, and at a very busy period on another platform, the workmen's train to John O'Gaunt would slyly sidle off behind an excuse for a J6.

The architecture of the line was pure Great Northern: centre-balanced somersault signals on wooden or latticed posts and handsome signal-boxes with their fretted barge-boards and finials. To me, it was evocative of a bygone age, for by the Fifties, an air of neglect had begun to take a hold on the line's Leicester terminus and the locomotives that serviced it.

Somehow, this state of affairs stopped short of the countryside outside of the city limits because the little stations along the line still revelled in a friendly rivalry for the best kept gardens and attention to the general smartness of the station was still a matter of great pride. Thurnby and Scraptoft, Ingarsby, Lowesby and John O'Gaunt were typical of the stations along the line towards Melton Mowbray and beyond, through the glorious landscape of the Vale of Belvoir by Scalford, Stathern and Redmile to the junction at Bottesford and a sharp right-hand turn towards Grantham. A journey along this line always seemed to be an endless and aimless meander that, if it were not for the natural beauty of the landscape in these parts, would have been an intolerable frustration. The train stopped every few minutes at one or other of the many stations with what seemed little or no ambition to continue, and in between, to the chagrin of anyone with an express to catch at Grantham, would stop in the middle of nowhere while the fireman cut across the fields to a nearby farm for a dozen eggs. The regularity of this charming exercise depended, of course, on the particular crew aboard the foot-plate. Of the stations themselves, there was little to choose between them – Thurnby and Scraptoft appeared to be similar to Ingarsby or Lowesby. Brick-built, they each served a tiny farming community and the architecture of their buildings was similar in both lay-out and design. Daily routine was about the same at each, as it might have been on any rural branch anywhere in the country, and as it had been for decades before.

The flower-beds at Lowesby were as well tended in 1953 as they were in 1923. The station-yard was wide, well swept and weed-free; the ornamental wooden fencing was a smart white echoed by that of the carefully painted line along the platform edge; and the lamp-posts, station canopy, stanchions, doors and windows glowed in the richness of their bright gloss paintwork. On a sunny day it was idyllic and in between trains was totally deserted. It was a place to 'stand and stare', to let one's imagination wander back over the years and imagine how it might have been at the turn of the century, say, or in the Twenties, or through the war years when anxious relatives waved off their loved ones into the unknown and the lamps and windows of the tiny waiting-room were blacked out and sightless.

The sounds of the countryside – the bleet of sheep and the birds overhead – dominated the surroundings, but as the time for the next train approached, people began to appear from nowhere – a porter, a man who seemed to be in charge (was he the stationmaster?), and a couple of passengers and then a third, all bound for Melton Mowbray. Two parcels were thrown onto a flat barrow, and a bicycle and a cat in a fishing basket were prepared for their outward journey. A whistle some distance up the line warned us all that business was about to commence and, as if by magic, a tired old J39 clanked into being with four of Mr Gresley's nice, if weathered, teak coaches in its wake.

The bustle of activity was short-lived. At the far end, the J39 sang like a

kettle, hissed a bit from a leaky safety-valve, but shut up so that we could hear a piece of coal being shovelled into the fire-box. In the middle, doors were slamming and heads were popping out of lowered windows, a voice shouted 'Lowesby' twice and at the back end a bicycle, two parcels and a cat were considered as a fair exchange for five milk-churns, a mystery object in a plain wrapper, and three baskets of pigeons.

And then it was all over. With a resigned sigh and a shrill short toot, the engine set off for pastures new and a repeat performance a couple of miles further on. Within minutes, the milk-churns were returned to their allotted space with several more, the pigeons cooed to each other on the flat barrow, and the mystery object quickly disappeared with the porter. Life was back to normal again, and there was not a soul to be seen on the deserted platform.

The thought that it might have been rather different twenty years earlier seemed to be a non-starter, except that the appearance and condition of the engine and its train would have been a better match to the pretty station and its well-kept gardens. But then, of course, the passengers would have been much more in evidence and even a bus might have been waiting in the station-yard, optimistic of a few fares, and perhaps a steam lorry belonging to a local haulier would have its boiler simmering gently while it was loaded up with the milk-churns for the various farms within the area. Behind some country stations were cattle pens for sheep and cows, and a siding, maybe into a coal wharf, where an engine might shunt contentedly for a few leisurely hours. Another station in a pretty part of the country might boast of a camping coach nearby, a smartly painted clerestory that had become a holiday home for country-loving pleasure seekers as an alternative to the boarding-house by the seaside.

I mulled over such thoughts of those old coaches being relegated to such use while I was sketching in Norfolk recently, when I unexpectedly came across a sad old carriage hiding in the undergrowth of a Norfolk creek. Ivy clung to its rotting wooden sides, in places encroaching on the musty interior. The old carriage stood, or perhaps one should say sagged, like a forlorn spectre of the glory that it no doubt once was.

It certainly looked as if it might have been part of the Great Eastern railway. My painter's eyes were revelling in the sight of the rot and the peeling, flaking paint, enjoying the rich little shadows that were thrown in the strong sunlight from the loose particles of old paint, making them stand out in a tromp l'oeil third dimension. It was thought-provoking to see all the cracks and splits in the weathered timbers that helped tell the story of this woebegone old-timer.

Now it is home to someone who lives within the cramped and damp walls of its much-travelled framework, coping with the leaks and the draughts of a North Sea wind on that remote spot on the Norfolk coast. Where did it travel, one wonders, and how did it come to land in that Norfolk creek? And how, in

'Last links with Tilton'
oil painting, 14in × 10in
The last run for an ex LMS Compound at Tilton in Leicestershire

Lowesby Station in 1953, the buildings in trim condition, and the little flower beds well tended and colourful

fact, will it end its life? Could it be that an angel of mercy in the form of a railway-carriage enthusiast will preserve it or will it continue to degenerate even further in the weeds of the Norfolk coastline?

Such a find is a great joy to a painter, for it is a subject full of character that not only makes a simple statement about the carriage itself but one that raises several questions in the minds of those who view the resultant painting.

The urge to paint the carriage was irresistible. The picture needed to be painted small, carefully and descriptively, in order that each crack and piece of flaking paint told the story in as graphic a manner as possible. I loved the little peep through the curtained windows at the wash-stand with its jug and bowl and the bed that hinted at the life lived on the other side of the rotting exterior, and the notice etched into the window – 'Smoking' – contrary to today's more usual 'No Smoking' signs. These details, together with the effects of the overall colours in the surfaces of the carriage and its great variety of textures, inspired me to choose that dilapidated old carriage as a subject for my canvas. It is always exciting to stumble across any piece of railway history

(page 70) 'Local at Thurnby'
oil painting, 30in × 20in
Thurnby and Scraptoft station on the Great Northern line out of Leicester

(page 71) 'No place like home'
oil painting, 12in × 10in

SMOKING

WESTON. 1984.

Allotments by the railway
Melton Mowbray.

Pencil sketch for 'Down the Lotty'

or architecture, no matter how humble, because it will have a story to tell and whenever I am anywhere near a railway line my eyes constantly search for subjects of this nature.

Railway territory means to me everything from a magnificent piece of railway architecture to an allotment shed with no more than a distant pall of smoke to link it with the railway. The atmosphere is all-important: the hint that just over that fence there is the line, the passing trains, and everything else that goes with the railway scene. Many of my subjects in this direction are no more than a glimpse, an attempt to make the viewer want to see more: it is the art of suggestion.

'Down the Lotty' is such a painting. Railways and allotments have always gone hand-in-hand, miles of allotments running along the length and breadth of the railway systems of the land.

It is pleasant to recall the long hot summer days of my boyhood when the hours were lazed away on the allotments by the side of the old Great Central line north of Leicester at Belgrave and Birstall, as the old men toiled in the sun, hoeing and digging, and straightening their aching backs to retire to the shade of their little retreats with their fusty smells of apples, soil and potatoes.

I lay in the long grass listening to the buzzing of bees and entranced by the fluttering butterflies busy among the wild flowers that grew in great profusion all around. The other sound, the one particularly waited for, was the 'clonk'

of the distant signal which heralded an even more distant exhaust beat. What was it? A Sandringham or a V2? I waited in anticipation to see if my guess was right and then would enjoy the excitement of the moment as the engine rushed past. There were moments when a war-weary WD came around the bend when I wondered if the anticipation had not been better than the event.

Some years later, while I was sketching on the allotments just by the Midland line at Melton Mowbray, I recalled those days, for there, as I drew some ramshackle old sheds, was the distant plume of smoke beyond a bridge over the line in the adjacent cutting. From that viewpoint, I knew that I would never see the locomotive, only hear its passing and maybe savour the smell of the smoke that would inevitably drift across the allotments as I worked. So that is the scene I depicted: tumble-down sheds, a rusting water-butt, some old iron fencing and the distant plume of anticipatory smoke, and to me it is as much a railway painting as any that are full of locomotives.

Painting is not simply a matter of recording fact – a photograph will do that accurately and quickly – it is the depiction of a personal view. A painting should have something to say, something that makes the viewer feel more than admiration for a painter's technique. It should be alive – something a photograph can never be, no matter how artistic the treatment. A successful

A4 at Gleneagles
oil painting, 30in × 20in
The best of both worlds for a landscape painter – beautiful scenery and steam at speed

painting – and it does not have to be a work of genius – will convey its message and have the power to draw the viewer back again and again when it will always have something new to offer.

Every painting is not successful, of course. Success in art is controlled by inspiration and if an artist feels inspired by his subject, then almost certainly the finished painting will reflect his inspiration. Inspiration, however, cannot be faked; it is the trigger that sets off an excited response of the senses so that an artist can express on canvas his feelings, ideas and responses to what he has seen or conceived.

Don Breckon creates many of his subjects; for example, his view of a Great Western scene in the Twenties will have been inspired by his vast knowledge of the subject, by looking at an old photograph or a television programme, or by hearing an idea – not, in fact, by seeing the scene in reality. Having created the picture entirely in his imagination, an inspired painting will result.

This happens in my experience also when painting periods of history from previous years, one must have the ability to visualise the end result. Sometimes of course the completed painting does not measure up to the initial vision despite the inspiration but that can be due to the deficiencies of one's painting technique.

The sort of sudden inspiration that came as I was travelling southwards through Nottinghamshire on the M1, when I saw a little piece of railway territory just off the motorway, resulted in a painting entitled 'Sundown'. The visual effects excited me so much that I wanted to express my feelings for it on canvas as soon as possible.

The wonderful effects of a winter sun are frustratingly transient, so the images reflected in the painting came together in reality for only a brief few moments. The great fiery ball of the sun dropped dramatically behind the silhouette of the power-plant and in turn reflected its colour into pools of cold dank water in the foreground. This magic scene was enhanced by the lumbering form of a Stanier locomotive reluctantly clanking through the landscape and giving a powerful and emotive centre of interest to the industrial scene.

I viewed this inspiring scene for only a few seconds as we sped along the road, yet it remained imprinted on my mind as sharp as the first few moments that I saw it. There was no time to sketch it, only precious moments to revel in and absorb the glory of a brilliant transformation by nature of an otherwise dreary winter landscape. An artist could ask for little more than a scene of such dramatic effects of light and colour, into which he can depict one of the last working engines of the steam age against a setting sun.

Light has been the inspiration of many of the railway subjects painted in

'Down the Lotty'
oil painting, 14in × 10in
The inevitable line-side allotments, ramshackle and untidy but full of character and colour, and in the distance the plume of smoke heralding the approach of another train to clatter past, its drift of smoke assailing our nostrils with its distinctive aroma (Jessop Collection)

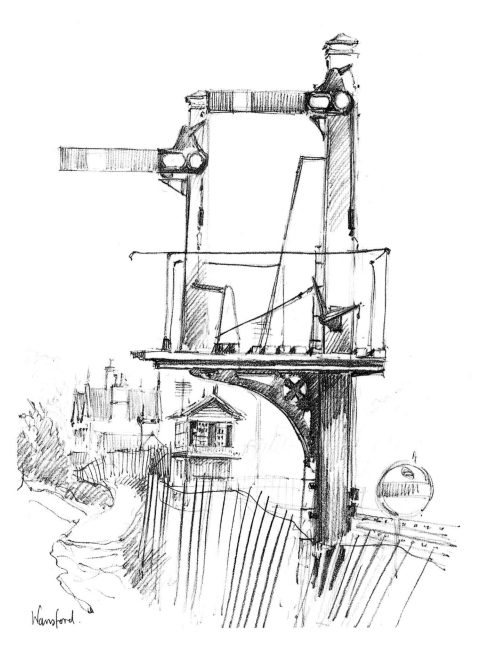

Station approach, Wansford, Nene Valley (pencil sketch)

(page 76) 'Sundown'
oil painting, 14in × 10in

(page 77) 'Sizzling Steam'
oil painting, 16in × 12in

75

recent years. I regard light as the most important factor in any painting and it has long since been a motivation for my pictures. Turner looked to the light for his inspiration and some of his most successful works were painted looking directly into the sun.

The imagery of an engine-yard was always for me at its most exciting either at dawn or at sunset, especially when I was directly facing the sun. The silhouetted shapes of engines against a low sun, their masses broken or softened by wisps of steam and drifting smoke, were as exciting as anything the railway could offer. 'Sizzling Steam' is an example; it is not concerned with the nuts and bolts of the engines, but with their masses and how they are affected by steam and smoke and light reflection. The atmosphere is all-important.

The atmosphere of the railway scene is for me also created by the wide variety of architectural delights – everything from signal-boxes or stations to a humble plate-layer's hut can be looked on with an eye for picture-making. The range of railway architecture is enormous and covers the entire range of nineteenth-century styles, mock-Tudor and Jacobean, Gothic and classical. The railway companies knew no bounds in their quest to make their buildings impressive and became patrons of the architects of the day, some of whom were among the most notable in the land. From the massive termini to the many delightful country branch stations, styles are many and varied, as are the materials from which they were built. Usually, local stone or brick would have been used, but wood was often used to good effect in examples like Petworth in Sussex, built by the London, Brighton and South Coast Railway. A long low single-storey structure with a low-hipped roof, it was clad entirely in timber around the top and below the corbelled eaves, there was a frieze decorated

Sketch for 'Landscape at Dent'

'Mist and Dereliction'
oil painting, 14in × 10in
The last of a signal box on the Great Northern Railway at Leicester. Cool harmonies of blue and greys (Jessop Collection)

with an attractive herringbone or zigzag pattern and a similarly patterned dado at the bottom of the walls.

Another picturesque station on the Great Western line was the half-timbered black and white building at Kidderminster in Worcestershire. This delightful structure, its façade of intricate fretted barge-boards over the windows and central porch, and a glass storm-canopy supported on iron brackets to welcome the traveller, reflected the architecture of the region.

Close to my home, Stamford town station in Lincolnshire is a wonderful example of how the local limestone was used to great effect. There are echoes of the Victorian Gothic in its many turrets and decorative tower and a similarity with the nearby Burleigh House. A simpler example a mile or two distant was the lovely limestone-built station at Ketton and Collyweston, with its local slate roof, bell-tower, and pretty bay-window looking on to the platform. These delights, countrywide, are too numerous to describe within the scope of this book, and I can do no more than mention a selection of my personal favourites here. Worthy of mention are such striking buildings as Great Malvern, a spa station with a superbly decorative Victorian Gothic clock-tower, and the low classical façade of the station at Ashby-de-la-Zouch in Leicestershire. Larger town stations like Huddersfield looked more like a stately home than a railway station, so imposing was the design for its colonnaded entrance, and the splendour of Bristol's Temple Meads with its Tudor Gothic forecourt buildings of chequered stonework and fanfare of turrets cannot be ignored.

Signal box at Dent.

Melton Station Box.
26-8-85

The Signal Box, Melton Mowbray (pencil drawing)

It would be wrong to pretend that I have painted pictures of all these beautiful structures, but I am conscious of their architectural appeal and importance. Unfortunately, many railway buildings have already been demolished and our heritage has dwindled dramatically over the last thirty years. In some cases, other uses have been found for station buildings worthy of preservation, and those at Monkwearmouth, the impressive Greek revival structure in Tyne and Wear, and the pretty royal station at Wolverton in Norfolk have both become museums, thus ensuring their future. Others, of course, particularly country stations, are now homes and, with tasteful modernisation, reflect their former use.

Signal-boxes have a style all of their own and many have featured over the years in my paintings. The Great Northern line out of Leicester had some attractive boxes, large and solidly built on brick bases with delicate barge-boards and finials. 'Mist and Dereliction' reflects one of these boxes after the decline of the line on a day of fine drifting mist, the architecture stark and vandalised but still reflecting the care that went into the original design of the cabin.

Melton Mowbray had an interesting and dramatic structure in the form of a cantilever signal-box supported high on iron stanchions. It was an unusual design on that line because it was of London North-Western origin rather than the usual Great Northern. All signal-boxes had great character, from those on the busy main line city stations to the lonely little structures on the Cumbrian fells. Those cabins at Shap summit on the Midland route north and Dent were a great personal favourite and I mourned the loss of the box at Dent when it was demolished a while ago.

Variations in the appearance of signal-boxes, like stations, depended on the railway company that built them and the local environment. There was almost a lovely signal cabin at Petersfield in Hampshire which was constructed entirely of glass, overhung with a delicate fancy canopy and topped with a small hipped roof, the whole structure cantilevered out on iron brackets from a supporting wall. There was the unmistakable style of the Great Central architecture throughout Leicestershire, and the great character of the simple wooden buildings of the halts at Ratby and Glenfield stations on the old Leicester-Swannington line, as well as the pretty toll-house there and the portals of the mile-long tunnel with the smallest bore in the UK.

Such attractions as the following were and still are great hunting grounds for railway subject matter: back-street terraces with no more than a hint of the railway behind them, engine-sheds, signal posts, gantries, and all the pieces of railway architecture that have fallen into decay. An overgrown and decaying

'A Ticket to Brooksby'
oil painting, 14in × 10in
The derelict Midland railway station between Leicester and Melton Mowbray

country halt can be very evocative, in contrast to those of smart appearance. 'A Ticket to Brooksby' is typical of any small station that has, by mere chance, escaped the demolition expert's hammer. These ruins stand as a melancholy symbol of defiance at Dr Beeching's axe which they did not escape. For the sake of an economic railway system, such country branches and their stations disappeared in vast numbers from our landscape, and with them went a way of life for the loyal servants who had dedicated their working lives to the service of the railway, apart from the detrimental changes that resulted for every small community that for almost a century the railway had served.

While walking around the deserted station at Brooksby, my foot kicked against a lump of rusting ironwork in the weeds, which, on closer inspection, proved to be a Midland Railway boot-scraper. This souvenir is now fixed out-side my studio door, serving the purpose for which it was designed in the days when Brooksby first opened its doors to local travellers. From under Brooksby Station's freshly painted canopy, a ticket might have been bought for the first stage of a journey to some far-flung corner of the Empire, or, as exciting to country folk then, a ticket for the half-a-dozen miles or so to the market town of Melton Mowbray.

The crunch of glass underfoot and the draughts that sneak through the derelict windows speak now of the neglect of our own times. The rails still gleam silver beside the overgrown platform, and thunderous inter-city expresses vibrate the very foundations of Brooksby's Victorian station on their rush from Birmingham to Norwich and back. But somewhere in all the progress that those inter-cities signify, lie more than a few tinges of regret in my romantic soul that no longer is it possible to buy 'A ticket to Brooksby', for the trains don't stop there any more.

Pencil drawing for 'A Ticket to Brooksby'

Brooksby Station.

7 STEAM IN TOWN AND COUNTRY

On the other side of the fence from the station platform in the early half of the twentieth century, steam played as large a part on the roads as it did on the railway lines of the countryside.

The steam lorry whose engine simmered in the station-yard as it awaited the arrival of the next train, carried off its loads to a diversification of businesses. Coal and coke would be trundled off by steam along the roads that radiated away from the station. In the towns, gas companies ran their fleets of steam wagons, and from breweries to builders' merchants, steamers were replacing the horse and cart in ever-increasing numbers. Steam-rollers also were a common sight, as they rolled the surfaces of roads that threaded both town and country. Massive and splendid showman's locomotives brought the fair to the village green, and from the other side of the hedgerows, polished engines gleamed in the summer sun as they effortlessly drove the threshing drum at harvest time. Also on the farms, powerful ploughing engines worked in pairs to haul the plough or cultivator through the earth.

Through a century of development from 1840 to 1940, the traction engine became a sophisticated and economic machine before it was superseded by the advancement of the internal cumbustion engine. Although the traction engine had threatened to replace horse-power, the horse itself had first helped to establish the machine, because the earliest traction engines were used to drive other machinery, and were horse-drawn in order to move them from one place to another. They were called portables and had a set of shafts at the front end.

Among the finest traction-engine manufacturers in the country were Thomas Aveling, Richard Garrett and Charles Burrell who formed their own companies. In the early years of development, Richard Garrett had designed and built a portable engine with a chain drive to motivate the wheels, thus making it necessary for the horse in the shafts to be used only for steerage purposes. A few years later, in 1860, Thomas Aveling developed an engine that required two men at the controls, one to look after the foot-plate and the other to steer at the front end.

So horse-power began to decline and with it came the first breath of the wind of change for the wheelwrights who for centuries had built carts and waggons for use in both agriculture and industry. At the turn of the century, there was a wheelwright's shop in every village of any size and most villages had a blacksmith's shop; sometimes wheelwright and blacksmith combined,

Pencil notes of Fowler agricultural engine No 14600 'Victoria'

as their combined skills were needed to manufacture a wooden vehicle. In addition, the blacksmith was farrier to a dozen or more different types of horse.

People believed that carts, traps, waggons and all other horse-drawn vehicles would continue to be built for decades to come, but although the wheelwright's occupation was threatened with the advent of steam power, the blacksmith's trade increased, for the new engine owners turned to the village blacksmith when their machines needed to be repaired. While the ancient craft of farriery did not die out completely, the blacksmith benefited most by servicing the new 'iron horse'.

The skill of pit sawyers was rendered obsolete with the emergence of the portable steam engine and its ability to drive a power saw. The steam-driven saw bench became a feature of every timber yard and teams of men with an engine and a van in which they lived became itinerant workers. They would arrive at the gates of wheelwrights' yards and cut up the trees into planks of the desired size and thicknesses with ease as the engine provided power for the saw that previously had required manual labour. While the sawyers faced a bleak future, their colleagues, the timber carters, benefited by the coming of steam on the road. A timber drag, used to cart the huge tree-trunks from the forest where they had been felled, was usually drawn by anything from two to six shire horses, but in difficult forestry and road conditions they might strain to maintain progress. One traction engine, however, could easily do the work of six horses, and more economically.

As a painter, I have been interested in all these aspects of the horse-drawn era, and next to my studio in the garden is a complete reconstruction of a country wheelwright's shop and forge. It has become a fascinating quest for me to form a collection of the tools and workshop equipment of the wheelwright's and blacksmith's trades as an extension of my interest in depicting the horse-drawn age on canvas.

It was a great thrill some years ago to find a Ruston Proctor portable engine of 1888 working a saw bench in a country wood-yard. A rough cover had been built over the driving belt to protect both the belt itself and the men working the saw. It reminded me of another wood-yard in a Leicestershire village that I often visited as a boy where the engine was kept in immaculate condition. It was great fun to play hide-and-seek in the large stacks of timber and I would look in awe and wonder at the little steam engine with its tall chimney extension and gliding pistons.

The same yard also ran a Foden steam lorry. Steam lorries were of two distinct types: the overtype and the undertype. The overtype carried its works over the top of the boiler and the undertype was below. Foden's had been building their overtype lorries, or waggons as they were called, from 1900, and they quickly became popular and successful. Foden's had been building traction engines at their Sandbach works in Cheshire since 1884 and phased out their manufacture only after the success of their steam waggon. The latter were built in a similar form until the 1930s and to cater for the demands of forestry and saw mills a derivative of the design was built in the form of a timber tractor.

There were many other builders of steam waggons, but beside Foden's the most prominent were Sentinel's of Shrewsbury whose waggons were used by a variety of trades. Sentinel's were favoured in particular by county councils to assist in the construction of road-surfacing work. A typical scene on a country lane would be of the steam lorry loaded with grit or broken stone, the tar barrel heating up the liquid tar ready for spraying, and the steam-roller waiting its turn to roll the road surface flat. The early Macadam roads were constructed by the application of a surface coat of tar over a foundation of water-bound broken stone, which was rolled and crushed by the roller.

The aroma of the tar barrel with its coal-tar smell was always an attraction and together with the steam lorry and the roller, provided free entertainment for countless hours. The smells of hot oil, steam and tar were a part of the attractions of my boyhood as I followed the steam lorries on my bicycle. In Leicester, they were usually bound for the gasworks in Navigation Street. Sparks flew from their chimneys and hot cinders fell onto the road in front of my wheels as I pursued them towards the entrance of the towering gasometers. I discovered that there was a wide variety of types and makers of these machines whose lorries could be seen frequently in the streets during the Forties. Perhaps the ultimate in steam-lorry design appeared in 1933 when Sentinel's developed a sophisticated steam lorry known as the Super Sentinel which was capable of speeds of up to 55mph. It was so modern in appearance that, but for a small chimney and the resulting smoke, it could

'Fiery Elias' under repair at Newbold Verdon

'The Forge'
oil painting
An engine built by Ransomes, Sims and Jeffries of Ipswich awaits
attention at the blacksmith's shop whilst all around are remnants of the
horse-drawn era, wooden wheels, wheelstools and the clutter of the anvil
and forge

well have been mistaken for a diesel-engined lorry.

It is little wonder that, having been brought up within the atmosphere of these steam years, I have made these machines the subject of so many of my paintings. As a boy, I always kept a watchful eye for a steam-roller at work and if I heard that one was in the area, I would cycle for miles across the city to see it. Steam-rollers were still at work until the 1950s and in 1957 I was prompted to do a large watercolour of one as I watched it at work in the city centre, as I realised that soon such a sight would no longer exist.

Marshall's of Gainsborough were prominent in the field of steam-roller design, as were others such as Fowler's, Robey's and Wallace and Steevens. My favourite designs came from the Rochester works of Aveling and Porter whose distinctive crest of a rampant horse on the front saddle with the name 'Invicta' inscribed below could be spotted a street length away, and whether the engine boasted a canopy over its works or not, their handsome appearance held them high in my estimation of steam-roller design.

By 1870 Aveling's had become the leading builders of steam-rollers but it was with the development and use of asphalt from Trinidad's famous lake that a new series of 6-, 10-, and 15-ton machines were built by the company. By this time, these engines had such features as a heavy rimmed fly-wheel, geared transmission and slightly coned driving rolls to equalise the wear over the width of the roll. It had been proved that it was better to roll cambered roads towards the centre and that a number of passes with a lighter roller was better than fewer with a very heavy machine.

With the greater advantages of asphalt over the previously macadamised roads, Wallace and Steevens developed a supremely successful roller called the 'Advance'. Its greatest virtue was a new double high-pressure cylinder unit which eliminated the need for a fly-wheel and therefore enabled the machine to reverse without having to stop from the forward movement.

Most steam-rollers were kept in good order, cleaned and polished; their brasswork was made to shine and the mechanics keenly attended to. An engine that had been well looked after could give sixty years of good service so the care was worthwhile. Indeed, to prove the point, a very smart 10-ton Aveling and Porter engine that was built in 1882 and is now in the Birmingham Science Museum, can speak of its seventy-one years of working life.

From the painter's viewpoint, immense character was inherent in these engines as they simmered at the roadside with droplets of hot oil and water trickling over oily paintwork. The heat and steam, the fancy lining, brass trimmings and makers' plates were all a part of the attraction. Some engines had beautiful ornate crests on their boilers – those on the Marshall engines

'Sunlight and Steampower'
oil painting
A 5 ton Overtype wagon of 1904 delivers its load of barrels to the Royal Oak. Foden steam wagons were much used by breweries and by the turn of the century would have been a commonplace sight on the streets

My vigorous style of watercolour painting during the Fifties is reflected in this large picture (30in × 22in) of an Aveling and Porter steamroller at work in the streets of Leicester. Dated 1957 it shows the demolition of the Wharfe Street area

were particularly attractive against the deep rich maroon-red of their standard livery – and at the back end by the foot-plate a fascinating assortment of fire-irons, shovels, buckets, tea billies, jackets, caps and overalls always hung.

The men who worked the engines were of a special breed, and a good man ate, slept and lived for his machine. Many men regarded their engines as their own and the working day did not finish with the last bit of rolling. If the engine was to stand through the night the fire would have to be banked, the boiler left full and the ash-pan damper closed. Side-sheets were fixed in position to

(page 88) 'The Steamroller Men'
oil painting
The crew of an Aveling and Porter steamroller 'face the camera' as it were for a picture around the turn of the century. In the background the corner shop displays several old enamelled plates advertising Julian tobacco, Hudsons soap and Walnut plug, adding colour and atmosphere to a commonplace setting. Also, the Aveling and Porter works plate

(page 89) 'The Magnificent Marshalls'
oil painting, 54in × 36in
The handsome design of the Marshall Rollers and the splendid crest

Aveling & Porter Single Cylinder
Road Roller built 1894

By Royal Letters Patent
No 5659
AVELING & PORTER
LIMITED
ROCHESTER
KENT
England

10 Ton Roller of
the Twenties.

No.17.

MARSHALL SONS & Co. GAINSBORO' ENGLAND

Marshall Roller in the Colonies 1900s

12 Ton Roller - 1930s

5 Ton Roller - 1911

Neston 1960

cover the motion and foot-plate and a lid was placed over the chimney-top. Lamps at the front and rear also had to be tended.

In the morning, the first job to be done, often at first light, was to clean out the fire, the spaces between the bars having to be cleared with a long poker so that the air could penetrate. Any clinker was then cleaned out with the clinkering shovel. The fire would be swept back as far as the breast-plate to clear the fire-box entrance. This kept in the heat while the engine was warming up and prevented any dust that might come from the fire-hole from spreading. The fire having been cleared and tended, the sheets would be taken off and oiling up would begin as steam pressure slowly mounted.

It was a treat as a boy to discover an engine in the evening when the engine man and the road crew had gone, so that I had it all to myself. Then I would furtively draw back the heavy side sheet just enough to scramble aboard and enjoy a secretive orgy of delight at being so fortunate as to participate in the mysteries of the foot-plate.

How I wished in my younger years that I could climb up on to one of those foot-plates. Little could I know then, of course, that in future years life would offer ample opportunities to do just that and to express my feelings about these lovely machines on canvas.

There were several makers of showmen's locomotives. Fowler's and Burrell's were undoubtedly in the forefront with Foster's a close third. It is probably fair to say that Burrell's magnificent Scenic Specials were considered by most to be the Rolls-Royce of showmen's road locomotives: apart from their performance and technical advantages, they were aesthetically pleasing and the sight of one working at night, or at the head of a train of loaded fairground waggons, could be a greater attraction than the fairground itself.

During the Fifties, Pat Colin's fair in October would occasionally draw me as it made its annual pilgrimage to Leicester. For some years it found space on waste land close by the Navigation Street gasworks and the engines I drew at night on a drawing-board lit by a bicycle lamp supported on an aluminium arm were usually to be found in the darkest corner of the fairground against the backdrop and sulphuric smells of the gasometers. Almost all of those drawings were torn up years later because I believed they were lacking in quality. I was being over-critical and realise now how useful they would be to me in my current work. Only two old watercolours of fairground engines remain in my collection of early works and they were done on the spot at night in 1954 after the October fair had moved its site to the Melton road on the city outskirts. One, a close-up of the front wheels and boiler of Pat Colin's No 1, is well recalled, because I sat down to get as low an angle as possible on the machine and had almost finished painting when a girl staggered around from the other side of the coconut shy and was promptly sick all over me, although fortunately the painting was not damaged.

The fairground was always a marvellous source of subject matter to paint. In the Fifties, some ancient old buses were converted for use as storage vehicles or even as living accommodation, but it was the beautiful old waggons that people lived in that really took my eye. If I could get past the inevitable fierce dog that lurked in the dark corners under the belly of the waggon, it was a treat to peep inside and see the cut-glass mirrors, the rich painted and carved ceiling, the fine china ornaments, and the glowing ruby reds of the oil lamps that gently lit their interiors. I longed to step inside one of those cosy and fascinating saloons, but never dared to ask.

The exteriors of these waggons were also of great charm, with their carved panels, cut-glass windows, a clerestory roof and ornate steps leading up to the stable-type door. My fascination with these homes and my inability to enter one led me years later to become a proud owner of such a waggon.

It was in 1970 that a woebegone and rotting Orton and Spooner veteran came my way. Built in 1900 it was, and now is again, a classic of its type. Indeed, it has all those lovely features that so attracted me in my youth, and now fully restored takes pride of place in the garden of 'The Lazy Acre' just across the lawn from the studio.

The waggon had belonged to the Gray family – East Anglian showmen – and was originally horse-drawn. Its very small wooden wheels allowed it to travel between towns on a flat transporter on the railway, so on the window of the entrance door is engraved 'private carriage'. The interior is beautifully fitted out with built-in mahogany furniture, bevelled mirrors with cut-glass star designs in their centres, and the ceiling too is carved, with mirrors inset to reflect the light. There is a saloon and a tiny bedroom that defies the knowledge that in addition to Rabby Gray and his wife, the years saw six children born within its 20ft long interior – five boys and a girl, Violet. It was from Violet that I learnt much about the old waggon's history after it had appeared on a television programme about my life as a painter and my interest in restoring it to its former glory. Both Mary and myself have a great love for the waggon and feel that it has well repaid the effort and care that we have taken over its restoration during the years since it first entered our lives.

Occasionally, especially on a summer's evening I will sit inside the saloon and imagine the waggon's slow progress behind the horse, and how, in later years, it would have been part of the train of waggons at the rear of a showman's engine. I wonder where it went in the early 1900s and about the fairs it attended, and what life was like for the travelling showman when the fair on the village green was an event of excitement and importance.

During the nineteenth century and well into the early years of the twentieth, the village green was at the heart of village life, and where better could the travelling showman display his varied delights than on the green with its backdrop of cottages, the church and inn?

The tradition of holding festivities on the village green dates back to medieval times and even further, but perhaps one should remember that originally fairs were trading events which people attended primarily to sell, barter for, or exchange goods. The entertainment provided by the travelling showmen

'The Griffin' Burrell Showmans locomotive at Shoby steam fair in 1968 (ink drawing)

BURRELL Nº 2804.   BUILT AT THETFORD 1906.

OH 2542

WESTON.

THE GRIFFIN.
SHOBY STEAM FAIR 1968.

The Orton and Spooner showman's wagon now fully restored at The Lazy Acre, resplendent in green and gold livery

The interior of the saloon in the showman's wagon, mahogany built-in furniture and cut glass mirrors reflect the colours of the carved ceiling. Through the door at the far end is a small bedroom

became increasingly popular with country folk whose pleasures were simple and few.

The fairgrounds of Edwardian England and for a decade or two beyond, were a celebration of the carver's and the painter's arts which had reached the pinnacle of their exuberance. Each ride, stall or side-show was a veritable palace of baroque carving and rich colour and it is little wonder that the engine manufacturers of the day echoed this ornate extravagance in the twisted brass canopy supports and the intricate lining of the showmen's tractors, and in the magnificent 'scenic special' road locomotives.

In 1889 the South Wales showman Jacob Studt ordered a road locomotive from the Thetford-based firm of Charles Burrell. His specification was for an attractive full-length canopy and decorative brass fittings, including fancy crests on the side-plates. This was how Burrell's began to make a speciality of such showmen's engines and soon fairground owners competed to own the most ornate or most magnificent example. Mr Studt was also the first showman to generate electric lighting and his showman's engine was possibly the first to have the dynamo fitted on its extended platform in front of the chimney. The dynamo was, of course, driven by a belt from the fly-wheel.

The sheer size and power of the larger engines enabled them to pull enormous loads, and trains of up to eight loaded waggons of rides, stalls and equipment were to be seen on the roads during the Twenties and Thirties. Even as late as the 1950s, loads of three or four waggons were still being moved from one location to another behind steam, and the frustration of being caught in a never-ending tail of traffic for miles on twisting roads behind the lumbering progress of an engine and its load is unforgettable.

The opportunity to sample the pleasures of the showman's foot-plate on the road came after I was commissioned to produce a large oil painting for that enthusiastic engine owner, Richard Preston of Potto in Cleveland. The pride of the Preston collection is the beautiful Burrell showman's locomotive *Lightning* of 1913, resplendent in an apple-green livery with red, black and gold lining.

Richard's late father Dick was an engine man born and bred. He worked for many years with engines in agriculture and started his own contracting business in 1933, carrying out threshing and forestry work. It was in 1956 that Dick bought *Lightning*; he paid £300 for her and intended to keep her as a

'All the Fun of the Fair'
oil painting
The superb Burrell special scenic road locomotive generates power for the rides at a summer fair sometime in the 1930s

hobby (rallies had just begun to be held at that time). However, a local brick merchant saw the engine and asked Dick if she could haul bricks. It was at the time of the Suez crisis when fuel was in short supply, so *Lightning* was put to work for three months on haulage duties. It was to be the start of Dick Preston's career as a haulier, and the thriving business that his son Richard now runs with his wife Anne boasts a fleet of no less than one hundred and forty splendid lorries, and earned for Anne the distinction of becoming the first lady chairman of the long-distance group of the Road Haulage Association of Great Britain, and the considerable honour of an MBE in 1987 for services to road transport.

Masham rally was to form the background for part of a film being made about the set of nineteen multi-image canvases painted in the late Seventies that together formed a chronological sequence on the development of the traction engine. They were sponsored by Bill Ford, a businessman with an interest in steam and one-time owner of the Jubilee class railway locomotive *Leander*. The paintings enjoyed a two-year tour of the UK and all the traction-engine pictures reproduced in this book have been taken from sections of those canvases.

The film required me to record a number of sequences with various engines, and it was Dick Preston's suggestion that I should drive *Lightning* into Masham for a few shots. It was the first time that I had actually travelled on the foot-plate on the road and I have to admit that I experienced a certain amount of fear, because from the great height of the engine, overtaking motor cars appeared to vanish totally out of sight beneath us. It was an experience I shall never forget and one of the resulting shots in the film was a distant view of *Lightning* crossing the river-bridge as I opened her up, with a belting black exhaust shooting high into the sky. The whole scene, reflected upside-down in the still water, made a picture fit for any canvas, and the knowledge that it was myself up on the foot-plate was self-satisfying as I remembered my boyhood and youthful dreams.

Even the short run into the centre of Masham was sufficient to give me a good idea of the power these huge engines contained, and I wondered as we trundled along what it must have been like to have had half a dozen waggons in tow and how enormous was the responsibility placed on the engine men in charge of such loads.

There were, of course, smaller loads to be moved on the roads and smaller engines provided suitable motive power. These were commonly called tractors and the Andover firm of Tasker's made a 'Little Giant' that weighed about 2½ tons; Foster's 'Lincoln Imp' was of similar proportions and weight. Most other tractors were a little larger and weighed about 5 tons. They had good acceleration and could haul loads of up to 20 tons. Unlike the larger road locomotives, the tractors were mainly iron tyred, but there were exceptions, usually on engines bought by showmen who preferred rubber tyres.

General-purpose traction engines were also used for agricultural as much as for haulage work, and it was in the harvest fields of late summer that these engines came into their own. The introduction of threshing machines revolutionised the harvest routines, so by the 1860s there were contractors with engines and threshing drums who would come for three or four days' work and help a farmer who could not afford to keep an engine and drum that would otherwise stand idle for most of the year.

Threshing is the climax of the harvest and until the invention of threshing tackle, the corn was laid out on the smooth floor of a barn and the grain was threshed out with flails. The latter were a type of stick that was hinged in the centre and two men worked in unison continuously beating the corn. It could be a winter-long task and it was little wonder that speedier and mechanised methods were found. With the new tackle, the crop from 30 acres of corn could be threshed out in one day.

There was always a great deal of excitement on the farm the day that the threshing tackle arrived. It would be accompanied by a small group of casual labourers who found work with the job and which they called 'sheenin'; about a dozen of them would be needed to cope with the variety of jobs on the corn-stack, with the drum and in the making of the straw-stack.

Sometimes a van for their living accommodation accompanied the team. Plain and sparsely furnished, the van was used by the men who preferred to sleep on the job; others might bicycle home, depending on distance and the fact that a 6.30am start was more often than not expected.

With the engine and drum drawn up beside the corn-stack to be threshed, the engine man, who was in charge of the whole operation, including the drum, elevator or chaff cutter, would make ready his engine. With enough pressure raised in the engine, the driving belt would be slipped over the fly-wheel to the drum in readiness and, with oiling up completed on both the engine and the drum, work could commence.

The sheaves were thrown into the mouth of the drum by the feeder standing on the drum's platform. He was dependent on the corn from the stack being passed to him by the band cutter who had in turn received it from the forks of the two pitchers working in unison on the stack. A steady swing was necessary to maintain an even supply into the drum otherwise it would cause the engine to splutter. The threshed straw fell from the drum into the elevator. This could be altered in pitch so that as the straw-stack grew, it would provide the men who were building the stack with a steady supply. The building of the straw-stack was usually a job for the more experienced or elderly men. It had to be done properly, and the work was less demanding physically than that of the pitchers.

At the end of the drum nearest to the engine, the grain trickled into sacks that were attached by hooks to the drum. It took two or three men to control this part of the sequence. The sacks hung beneath a series of four trap-doors, so when a sack was full the trap-door above it was closed and its neighbour

'Threshing in the 1890s'
oil painting
An Alchin threshing engine drives the drum at harvest time and an
Alchin cylinder block

opened, thus maintaining a steady flow. Two trap-doors were worked this way, the full sacks being taken away to be weighed, while the other two doors were used for the small weed seeds and low-grain corn that had been graded by a series of sieves inside the drum.

As the drum worked, it emitted a deep hum, and as it vibrated and shook, it created a dry dust. The chaff boy's job was to bag up all the tiny pieces of straw and husks that blew down the chute. This had to be done within the restricted space between the drum and the corn-stack, a dirty and dangerous job because of the moving wheels and belts on the side of the machine.

It is little wonder that the first priority of the workers' lunch-break was to slake the thirst of a dry, parched throat. The half-hour break was usually around 9am, when bacon or cheese sandwiches, or maybe a slice of fat salt pork, was washed down with cold tea.

The dinner-break was taken at 1pm for an hour, and the afternoon's work would finish between 5 and 6pm. It added up to about a twelve-hour day for men and boys alike, longer perhaps for the engine man who then had to bank up the fire and sheet up the engine for the night.

The long hours and back-breaking work for a meagre reward belie the romantic picture of the Edwardian harvest field as an example of 'the good old days'. Threshing was done only from late September, and was finished by the early part of the following year, which meant that both the engine men and drum workers needed to find work in other areas for the remaining months. One avenue open to them was steam ploughing in summer – another aspect of the contractor's work as he travelled from farm to farm. For this work, however, he would need a set of different engines and some contractors would own several sets of these expensive machines which always worked in pairs. As with threshing, the contractors might travel long distances, with the crews and the living accommodation alongside. They were paid for their work on an acreage basis, ploughing or cultivating at so much per acre, with the farmer supplying the coal and water. There were usually five men to a team, including a lad whose job was to cook meals in the accommodation van and to replace a man when he needed a rest. The days were long and arduous, with farmers preferring the work to be done before winter or during the spring.

The business of steam ploughing was pioneered by John Fowler, and his works at Leeds produced the powerful engines suitable for the job. The process began with an engine being set at each side of a field. Beneath the boiler of these engines was a winding drum, or clip drum, with up to half a mile of wire cable. The plough that was set between the two engines was attached at each end to these cables and could therefore travel back and forth across the field, ploughing the ground each way as it went. The team was split between the two engine drivers and two rough-riders on the plough itself. Co-ordination between the engine men and those on the plough was achieved by a system of whistle blasts which maintained the continuity of the operation. The foreman travelled on the plough, a five-furrow monster also manufactured by Fowler's, and at a blast on the whistle the slack on the cable was taken up and the plough began to move slowly away towards the engine at the far side of the

field. The sharp exhaust beat of a single-cylinder engine would echo across the fields in the crisp morning air, to the accompanying cries of the crows in the topmost elms and the swooping call of the gulls which insistently followed the progress of the plough.

With the plough at the far side of the field, the driver would give the foreman time to turn and then, with another whistle blast, would take up the slack until the plough's weight was felt, at which he would open up the throttle as the winding drum hauled the plough back in. As with threshing, the smooth nature of the continuous running of the operation was paramount to the excellence of the job and the economics of the operation.

When travelling on the road between farms, one engine would tow the accommodation waggon and water-cart, the other would haul the plough or cultivator. The arrival of the team of workers at a small village in the early years of this century must have been an event to stir the interest and imaginations of old and young alike, and no doubt the attraction of these majestic engines and the nomadic way of life the men enjoyed were incentives to any country-loving young boy to want to join them. Some of the older men, and the foreman or the engine man were probably attracted in this way as boys and went on to dedicate their entire lives to steam ploughing – an operation which continued on the farmlands of Britain until the late 1930s, when it gave way to the progression of diesel power.

As a painter of the age of steam and a witness in the Sixties to the demise of steam power on our railway systems, I realised that steam engines were no longer to be seen on the road, and their demise had gone unheralded and, for the most part, unrecorded. I felt as much sadness at the sight of a steam-roller or a showman's engine once the ravages of time had taken their toll as I did when I saw the lines of once magnificent railway locomotives in the breakers' yards. All the years of technological development, of expectation, and of pride on behalf of the companies who built them and the men whose lives were dedicated to working with them, were inherent in the stark vision of any of those rusting machines in the weeds of some forgotten corner of a farm or scrap-yard. They were symbolic of an age that had reached its obsolescence and had left behind a wealth of inventive technological progress that had added greatly to the country's respect and prosperity.

In the 1940s, a great many of these road-using engines were sold for scrap for as little as £10–£15. No thought was given to their preservation – and who could have foreseen in those days the enormous sums that are realised now as restored engines change hands? Much has been preserved for us to enjoy by private individuals, as the summer-time rally fields bear witness, but it is a sobering thought that as many as 90 per cent of the steam engines at work on the roads of Britain disappeared between 1946 and 1950, and even then it was difficult to imagine that, within a few more decades, steam on the railways would be following the same course.

'Ploughing Engines at Work'
oil painting

8 A MIDLAND MAN LOOKS WEST

It was approaching dusk as a simmering A3 stood at the platform end under the great arc of Newcastle Central's southern portals. A column of urgent smoke rose steadily out of the chimney and the constant scrape and ring of the fireman's shovel as the tumbling coal was spread over the fire confirmed that the engine was all but ready for the road. I climbed aboard and settled myself into a corner where I could watch the proceedings from the fireman's side of the foot-plate without becoming a nuisance to the crew. The fire was checked again and the shovelling continued; to an unfamiliar eye, it seemed to be an enormous amount of coal as it was thrown, shovelful after shovelful, over the spread of the fire, the deft movement of the shovel never once baulking the fire-box entrance. To feel the heat from that fire and sense the build-up of latent power was as exciting as it was being on the foot-plate of an express locomotive en route to York.

The familiar sounds of doors slamming, voices shouting, the rumble of empty parcel barrows and a final sharp, short blast of the guard's whistle somewhere down the platform, and we were off. The needle hovered over the red line on the pressure gauge, the fireman's attention to the fire having brought the boiler up to full pressure. The driver, a man of few words, had been leaning out from his window to observe the situation on the platform. He returned to his seat and, with a curt nod at his fireman, blew off the brake and reached for the regulator handle. For a few seconds, nothing appeared to happen, but then the whole of the foot-plate controls suddenly appeared to pulsate with life as the cylinders filled up with steam and, with an almost imperceptible movement, the great locomotive slowly began to haul its train out of the station.

Above the metallic grind of iron wheels on iron rails, the engine made a more positive beat as the regulator was opened up a notch. The 'thump, thump' under my feet told me that it was going to be a hard ride as the tender-plate ground and slid over that of the engine, and already it was necessary to hang on to the side as the fireman busied himself with an oily rag on the brass and copper of the controls; below us, the wheels were protesting at the criss-cross of lines with a persistent grinding and bumping. The side rods echoed off the cutting walls as the regulator was eased off to allow for the array of red lights ahead. The engine rumbled over the cross-overs, blew off steam in its impatience to get away and sidled out over the Tyne to the grind of the wheels, the hiss of steam coming from seemingly everywhere, and the indecipherable curses of the driver. 'We'll no get away yet, pet,' shouted the fireman, but as the reds changed to green, his mate's reply was a long pull on the A3 whistle and, as he finally opened the regulator, the majestic sound of a suddenly increased exhaust-beat sounded loud and clear from the chimney, adding to the deafening cacophony of sound aboard the foot-plate. The fireman tended his fire again and signalled to me to take his seat, so for the first time aboard a moving engine, I looked out at that special view along the length of the massive boiler, which was black against the last vestiges of light in the evening sky.

Lights flashed past and the tracks to the side of us were a blur of sleepers and reflecting metal. A glance back inside at the speedometer showed that we were already doing 60mph. The chimney shot its exhaust clear above us and I revelled at the sight of the red-orange sparks glowing hot against the mass of smoke and the darkness of the night. Leaning out a little, the sounds of the side rods, pistons and the huge wheels competed with the sharp bark of the exhaust as we were thrown and bucked on that oscillating foot-plate. Stations – a blur of light – shot past to the continuous scream of the whistle. The fireman continued to shovel, adding to the clamour, while the glow from the fire illuminated his figure in a fluorescent orange that spread over the foot-plate fittings and lit the roof of the cab so that the rivets and bolts threw elongated shadows across the dull orange glow of its surface.

So this was steam at 80mph; the thrill was tremendous and although I had taken my sketchbook on board, I was too involved with the experience to have even thought about drawing my impressions.

As with all foot-plate trips, it was over far too soon for me and the lights of York were fast approaching; the pace of the engine became slower, green lights dazzled ahead and as the build-up of tracks and signals, overbridges and cross-overs flashed past below us, the first signs that we were going to stop at York began to happen. The ear-shattering noises on the foot-plate were joined by those of the vacuum brakes being applied, and there was a loud suction sound as air filled the brake pipes.

'Eclipse'
oil painting, 54in × 36in
The end for a derelict roller in the undergrowth of a Norfolk contractor's yard

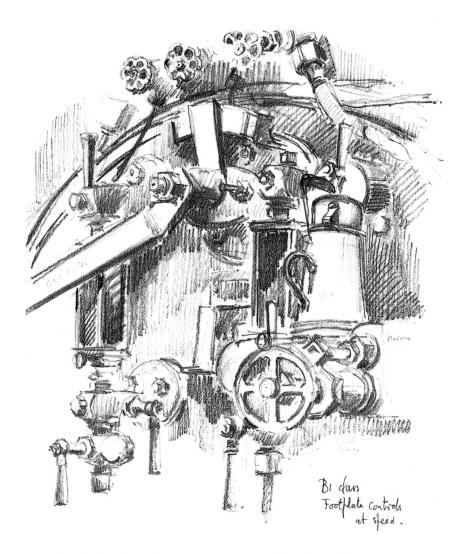

On the footplate of a B1, Leicester Central (pencil sketch)

Ivatt Atlantics at the National Railway Museum prior to its opening in 1975

The grinding below the wheels jarred through my body as we rattled at what seemed to be far too fast a rate into that most glorious of station interiors at York. As we slid around the curve to a halt, the driver, unsmiling and work-weary, checked his watch: 'One minute up, lad.' The fireman nodded his approval. It was time to get off and in climbing down onto the platform, the fireman, grinning, asked in his broad Geordie accent, 'Was it alright for you, pet?' Needless to say, my thanks were fulsome, but as goodbyes were said, I realised that my legs were still shaking, my back was as cold as ice and my head ached intolerably – but yes, you could say that it had been all right.

The excitement of that first foot-plate trip was tremendous, more so because it was on an A3, a class of engine that had always held my admiration, and the experience of riding on the foot-plate must surely have been, for anyone other than the seasoned professional, an emotional experience. Just how soon a fireman, new to the job, got used to it, is a matter for conjecture. Several steam drivers who left the railways on the cessation of steam operations felt that they could never face life in the cab of a diesel locomotive, nor were they averse to admitting that a life on the foot-plate was a cut above the ordinary way of life for a working man and that the initial thrill of the foot-plate remained with them all their life.

A number of the A3 class of locomotives were shedded at Leicester's Great Central depot during the 1950s, but it did not seem right to see these famous East Coast main line locomotives on the secondary route of the Great Central that ran from London's Marylebone Station to Sheffield and the North. The Leicester shed in the Fifties housed Bls, V2s and A3s, but the latter were transferred to Grantham in 1958, which brought about even more extraordinary changes as Midland region class 5s, Jubilees, and incredibly, Royal Scots, appeared in the yards. So, if the A3s had seemed strange to a man who had been brought up with the magic of the Great Central's Directors and Sandringhams, it was almost sacrilege to meet these giants of the LMS on such hallowed territory.

Perhaps it was the isolation of the Great Central's metals that gave it a wonderful individuality. The architecture of the line followed the same house-style of brick-built stations with handsome decorative brickwork and signboards with pretty ornate framing, attractive station canopies and iron-work, and blue brick overbridges.

The engines on the line in earlier years did not display a large variety of types and consequently I saw the same locomotives repeatedly, but the fact never bothered me; the Great Central was unique and that was part of its charm. Speed was another characteristic of the Great Central line with its long sweeping curves. The stretch of line between Aylesbury and the borders of Nottinghamshire was extremely fast, the engines of the B1 and V2 classes reaching speeds of 80 and 90mph. The Leicester to Nottingham run, which included the stretch of route now preserved by the Main Line Steam Trust, was particularly fine. The 23 miles were timed non-stop at 24 minutes, and with superb driving, were often done at the mile-a-minute timing.

The Great Central line was never modernised and it remained a steam

A4 at York
oil painting, 30in × 20in
LNER 4-6-2 'Silver Link' arrives at York in the spring of 1947

Schools Class locomotive under repair (pencil sketch)

railway almost to the bitter end, hence the run-down Jubilees and Scots, which the Great Central men with their customary fortitude and expertise coaxed along with some very respectable results. Steam survived until 1966, when a meagre diesel rail-car service was introduced between Rugby and Nottingham. The smaller stations were all closed which marked the inglorious end of a great line. The final whistle was blown on 3 May 1969.

What remains to be seen of the Great Central in Leicestershire is due entirely to the efforts of the Main Line Steam Trust, and the stations at Rothley, Quorn and Woodhouse, and Loughborough reflect much of what existed in the line's heyday. At the time of writing, plans are underway to rebuild the derelict station at Belgrave and Birstall on the outskirts of the city of Leicester – my favourite childhood train-spotting location – as the new terminus of the line. The station's desolate ruins have for the last two decades represented a forlorn spectre of past glory as they looked down a weed-grown road to nowhere. When the rebuilt station is complete and a gleaming B1 stands alongside the platform with its rake of coaches, I shall be there for the sake of a future painting and a private celebration at the tangible re-creation of a piece of my childhood.

The A3s that had left the Great Central to return to their more familiar territory of the East Coast main line stood once again in the familiar setting of Grantham shed. What had become old favourites, like *Gay Crusader*, *Royal Lancer*, *Enterprise* and *Merry Hampton*, were to end their days from this particular staging post on one of the fastest stretches of the route North.

The line through Grantham was indeed fast and the experience of watching the non-stop expresses taking Grantham Station by storm is unforgettable. The narrow platforms meant that even by standing well back, the blast could be frightening to say the least, and with the runaway effects of Stoke bank to the south, the speed and effect of a streamlined A4 thundering through with its chime whistle going full blast was the railway experience par excellence. There was of course a 70mph limit through Grantham, but not all drivers seemed to be aware of it.

Grantham shed had been the destination as a youngster of my journeys along the meandering stretches of the Great Northern line from Leicester. Always my heart thumped as I entered the darkness of the shed through the tiny doorway at the furthest end and was confronted by some of the greatest giants of the steam age in the shape of Mr Gresley's huge streamlined Pacifics that stood shoulder to shoulder with A2s and A3s. As a boy, the close proximity of these engines, some warming up as they gathered steam, was as exciting as it was frightening and I was always relieved afterwards to seek the sanctuary of the line-side allotments by the turntable. The volume of locomotives stationed in the yards at Grantham during the Forties and Fifties had to be seen to be believed. There was constant activity, with engines manoeuvring about, being turned on the turntable only yards from my favourite vantage point for watching the proceedings. It was here that engines were changed over on the expresses to the North and South that had stopped in the station alongside the yards.

As steam declined, so did my visits to Grantham. Many of the engines had become run-down and dirty – not that as a painter I cared too much about that, but Grantham, like the Great Central, had occupied a special place in my affections. I could never forget the spectacle of sparkling apple-green engines simmering majestically in the yard with their red and brass name-plates, and the most spectacular sight of all, those garter-blue streamliners that hurtled through the station with such power and speed, and that were surely the epitome of the glamorous age of steam. However, by September 1963 the shed was closed and the engines were scrapped at an alarming rate. Within weeks, the place was totally desolate as it waited for the final act of the demolition contractor's hammer.

The Great Central and the lines of the LNER were only one side to my being a 'Midland' man. The other, as far as Leicestershire went, was apparent in the network of the Midland route from St Pancras to the North. This was an extremely busy line, and the engine-yard and round-house at Leicester reflected this with an allocation of some eighty-five locomotives. The yard became another of my favourite places for both train-spotting and painting in later years. It was atmospheric and ideally situated for photography and, more importantly, for sketching. Swain Street bridge crossed over the lines between London Road Station and the great sprawl of the yard with the signal-box, coaling tower, ash plant and turntable backed up by the round-house beyond. The best view of all this was from the mesh-fronted walkway that extended from the bridge right around one side of the yard at an elevated position some 20ft above the lines of engines and the bustling activity of the yard. To be able to look down on all this and savour the smells that drifted up, apart from the enveloping steam and smoke from engines directly below, was surely every railway enthusiast's dream.

So it was for a budding young artist whose wet oil paint often collected more than a smattering of black smuts to add to the 'atmosphere' of the painting. The composition of the view took in the coaling tower and ash plant in a diminishing line of perspective and was therefore, pictorially speaking, as good if not better that any other busy railway yard in the country. The engines included the inevitable Stanier class 5s and 8Fs, Austerities, compounds, Stanier and Fowler tank locomotives, among sundry ancient Midland 0-6-0s, and if one were lucky, the odd Jubilee might stand proudly among their number, somehow head and shoulders above the rest.

As a youngster these were my favourite LMS types, their tapered boilers rich in Brunswick green with 6ft 9in driving wheels and the slender chimney that one learnt to distinguish from a class 5 at a distance of a thousand yards being the aesthetically pleasing aspects of their design. They were the greyhounds of express locomotives and their three-cylinder syncopated exhaust beat echoed

'Mallard at King's Cross'
oil painting, 24in × 20in
Gresley's superb A4 pulls away in spirited style

across the city outskirts as they built up speed on their journeys north or south of Leicester.

The exit southwards runs through deep blue-brick cuttings under over-bridges and the short Knighton tunnel towards Kettering, Bedford, Luton and the capital. Of the run northwards, the most important railway centre is undoubtedly Derby with its great history as the headquarters of the Midland Railway and a tradition of locomotive building that was second to none. The Midland Railway was incorporated in 1844 and for the next seventy-nine years built locomotives under the direction of four chief mechanical engineers; S. W. Johnson stands out as the designer of some very efficient and extremely handsome locomotives, among which was his beautiful single wheeler – one of the most glorious of all Victorian engines ever built – and his later three-cylinder compounds, a handsome and successful design. These were later modified by his successor R. M. Deeley, and their success was acknowledged by the building of another forty engines. The design was continued further in turn by Deeley's successor Sir Harry Fowler, who carried on building the class after the amalgamation of the Midland with the LMS.

The construction shops at Derby that built these splendid machines were still in full swing when it was my privilege to visit them with my father in the late Forties. My vivid impression was one of tremendous activity – there were engines in all states of construction and completion. There was so much to see in the massive interior that I was bewildered by it all: the unfamiliar sight of locomotives without their tenders; the unimpeded view of a foot-plate, its controls exposed, incomplete; a row of wheels straddling the track; step-ladders, work-benches, tools, equipment and fittings strewn everywhere; the incessant clamour of hammering and riveting; of men dwarfed by the immense size of the machines they were creating while others climbed over the half-built and anonymous giants of the steam age. The overhead gantry swung heavy sections of metal to and fro, seemingly just above our heads, and the illuminating flash of the welder's torch turned the deep shadows underneath the darkest recesses of those iron giants into a momentary kaleidoscope of extraordinary shapes and reflected lights. The mysteries of the birth of a locomotive – it was quite bewitching and unforgettable.

That visit to Derby was also the first time that my eyes had savoured the pleasures of a busy round-house. From the drifting smoke that licked around the ducts high in the roof to the exciting and bewildering display of Jubilees, Crabs and Patriots around the turntable, it was all redolent of the steam age at its zenith. The place was imbued with a sense of latent power; the immense activity of men at work presented a picture of Derby in its finest hours, proof enough of the great technology that from its Victorian beginnings had placed Britain among the most respected countries of the world. At the time of my first visit to Derby in 1949 the country was recovering from World War II and was building for a better future. The tremendous activity within the erecting shops confirmed that industry was indeed on its feet again, and the thought that the railways would always be the essential foundation of the success and stability of our industrial future seemed indisputable. That steam would continue to play its part in that future also seemed at the time to be beyond dispute. How could one imagine, therefore, that within another five years a modernisation plan for the railways would herald the phasing out of all steam traction and that within another decade the steam age would be over.

The glorious history of the Derby works and the engines that emerged from them was equal to anything in the annals of railway development. The Midland Railway had been the foundation of that success with its great designers and the guiding hand of Sir James Allport who became the general manager in 1853. He was later appointed to be a director and received his knighthood in 1884. His vision and exciting policies led the Midland forward. Well-devised and punctual services became a hallmark of the company, as did its attention to the comfort of passengers and the cleanliness of its rolling-stock and loco-motives.

By the 1860s it was apparent that to maintain those standards throughout the route to the north it was necessary that a main line over the treacherous uplands of the Cumbrian hills to Scotland should be built. The building of this line was the Midland Railway's crowning glory, and the Settle and Carlisle section, part of which became known as 'the long drag', was celebrated as an outstanding achievement in the history of railway construction. There was no precedent. Engineers had never before tackled anything like the terrain that had to be conquered on so vast a scale over the wilds of the Cumbrian moors and the ascent to Ais Gill summit at 1,169ft above sea-level. The line rose over the very spine of England and necessitated the building of no less than fourteen tunnels and twenty viaducts.

The line to the north was built at an immense cost to the Midland Railway and the loss of many lives, as witnessed by a memorial tablet in the tiny church at Chapel-le-Dale. The real tribute to the engineers and the thousands of navvies who were employed to build the line lies in such viaducts as the quarter-mile-long Ribblehead, over 100ft high and built of stone that came in 8-ton blocks, which had to be manoeuvred and lifted by leverage and block and tackle. At Dandry mire, for instance, the peat simply swallowed up every scrap of tipped material, which should have risen as an embankment, until eventually a ten-arch viaduct had to be built instead.

The problems must at times have seemed insurmountable; tunnnels such as those at Rise Hill and the infamous Blea Moor had to be burrowed through solid rock. Blea Moor alone cost many lives and drove men mad with fear so that they could never go underground again. Even today it is a fearful place – a black, dank hole where the ghosts of Victorian navvies can in an unrivalled flight of the imagination whine a chill and forbidding warning on the wind.

The line was eventually completed and opened in 1876. It had been conceived and built out of a spirit of competition with the LNWR, whose lines had forged the West Coast route to Scotland, and also with the Great Northern,

'Black 5 at Wild Boar Fell'
oil painting, 16in × 12in
Stanier's magnificent all-rounder does battle with the ascent of Ais Gill

whose routes travelled northwards on the eastern side. As a result, it was brilliantly designed and magnificently engineered, and was recognised as the most spectacular piece of railway construction in the British Isles.

Whenever I visit that part of the country now, over a century after the construction of the railway, I cannot help but remember all that went into its creation, and whenever a painting is produced of any particular aspect of the Settle to Carlisle line, the history becomes as important to me as the composition of the landscape.

Among my favourite stretches are the tracts of countryside between the peaks of Pen-y-Ghent and Ingleborough where Ribblehead viaduct crosses the valley, the area of Blea Moor, with its isolated signal-box and tunnel, Arten Gill viaduct and Dent Head viaduct on the approaches to Dent station; all have been painted many times, both for myself and to commission. The vast sweep of Dent's landscape is so superb that for a painter who is as happy painting open landscape as he is railways, it is the perfect blend. Beyond Dent, the rails northwards pass through Moorcock tunnel and out over the Lunds viaduct, only to plunge directly into Shotlock tunnel and emerge close to the wild summit of Ais Gill. The entire area is so paintable, whether it is seen in summer sunshine or winter ice and snow, although the winter landscape is artistically more dramatic.

It was always a special experience to be at Dent with the sounds of nature and the wind whistling in the telegraph wires, and then to hear far-distant, perhaps almost imperceptibly at first, the rhythmic beat of a hard-working locomotive, its sound borne across the valley only to vanish again on the wind, and then to return a little louder in the steady approach to Arten Gill viaduct. Then suddenly she would appear, magnificent, a huge plume of smoke being scattered by the wind across the moor to the long wail of a Brittania whistle as the engine and its train approached Dent Head viaduct for the sweeping curve towards the station. With it came a climax of deafening sound as the engine roared past and through the station to drive under the road-bridge, its beat bouncing off the cutting, echoing into the distance on its climb to Ais Gill. It was a prolonged and emotive train-watching experience and the essence of the line that has become not only a remarkable legend, but stands as a lasting tribute to the skills of the Midland Railway, its engineers and the toil of the navvies who worked in such harsh conditions to complete the work.

Sitting by Dent, sketching, with the view of the two viaducts, I have often thought that the sight of a Johnson Single, perhaps double-headed, approaching with a rake of beautiful clerestory or Pullman coaches in their Midland lake livery, must have been glorious indeed. It must have looked sensational in its day.

The opening of the line led to the introduction to this country of the Pullman carriage built in the United States of America and of a standard unequalled by any other company at the time. As they equalled their rivals, the Midland led the field again with better dining cars, sleeping cars, and the overall comfort of their saloons.

For a final look at the history of this great railway, one must return to the beginning and to Leicester, to a line that has the distinction of being the first steam-operated railway in the Midlands.

The Leicester and Swannington was opened in 1833, engineered by Robert Stephenson to serve both passenger traffic and the needs of the Leicestershire coalfields. This historic little line was absorbed into the Midland Railway in 1846 to become the oldest part of the company. Its Leicester terminus was at the West Bridge Station close by the canal and the lift bridge that was described in Chapter 1 (see p13).

It was my pleasure to see this almost-forgotten line over the years. It was still being operated by some antique Midland 2F 0-6-0s right up to 1964. Each had a narrow cab, some with the original Johnson cabs, others with the Deeley rebuilt version, that suited the particularly small bore of Stephenson's mile-long Glenfield tunnel. Very few engines could even gain entry into this, and later classes (BR Standard class 2) had to be rebuilt with narrow cabs to enter, and even then it was extremely tight.

The little station at Glenfield with it wooden waiting-room stood derelict for many years, as did its twin at Ratby. Glenfield, with its adjacent coal-yard was very paintable and drew me back many times. Passenger trains no longer ran – in fact, the Leicester West Bridge Station had closed to passenger traffic as early as 1928, but twice a day a freight train, mainly coal, would trundle along at a leisurely pace through the old tunnel on its way from Desford, and this continued until the line closed in 1966 – 133 years after Robert Stephenson had built it.

My submersion since childhood in the operations of the LMS and with it the various remnants of the old Midland Railway prevented me from looking further afield in the heady days of the LMS and the early years of British Railways. The tremendous excitement of the West Coast main line was readily available for the sake of a train-ride at both Rugby and Nuneaton. At the latter, I watched the original Patriots and Royal Scots, and the beautiful streamlined Pacifics racing down the bank to rush through Nuneaton Station with a blast greater than any it had heard through the war years, and in contrast, to look in fascination as the last of the ancient LNWR 4-6-0 Prince of Wales class engines, *Queen of the Belgians*, trundled around the bend on her daily trip to Leamington Spa. Of the same class, No 25673 *Lusitania* shared this duty.

At Rugby, as the years went by, my response to the aggressive appearance of the rebuilt Scots and the sheer magnificence of the most powerful of all of Sir William Stanier's designs, the Coronation class Pacifics, was apparent in sketch-form; Stanier was, in my opinion, one of the greatest, if not *the* greatest, of the chief mechanical engineers of the twentieth century. His Coronation class both in its streamlined and semi-streamlined form was the epitome of power and aesthetic design; everything I sensed in the steam locomotive was embodied in the majestic pile of this locomotive.

Landscape at Dent
oil painting, 40in × 20in
No engines, just the sweep of the hills as we wait for the distant beat

GLENFIELD STATION
1965.

WESTON.

Sir William Stanier came to the LMS from the GWR and put much of his Great Western ideas and experience into the engines he built. In his rebuilds of the Patriots, Scots and Jubilees, the Great Western influence is easily traceable; not that the LMS ever went in for anything as decorative as a copper-capped chimney or very great elegance, but for handsome locomotives whose aggressive design expressed the sheer power of steam, the LMS under Sir William Stanier's direction was unrivalled.

Freight at Dent Station
oil painting, 40in × 30in

'Glenfield Station' Derelict and nearing closure of the line in 1965. This watercolour (22in × 15in) was painted on site on a day of intermittent drizzle during that year

The copper-capped engines of the Great Western did not feature largely in my younger years and it was not until much later when a sketchbook superseded my Ian Allen stock-book, that my experience of these engines became much wider.

The link for a Leicester lad in the late Forties lay at the Great Central Station where the connection to Banbury often brought a Great Western

111

Hall class on either freight or passenger duty into the heart of the Midlands and beyond. Summer holiday traffic could bring a surprising variety of Great Western engines through on their trips from York or Sheffield to Bournemouth, Sheffield to Cardiff, or Newcastle to Swansea.

Halls, Manors and County class locomotives might be viewed on the Great Central's lines and sometimes there was even a visit on relief duty by an engine from the southern region. It was not unusual for inter-company working to be practised on the Great Central, and the York to Bournemouth would be headed by a Central engine as far as Banbury, a Western engine taking over from there; the procedure would be reversed on the return journey with a Great Western engine working up to Leicester. The Bristol to York night mail was worked by Swindon men, and summer Saturday workings of the Cardiff to Sheffield run also saw the Great Western men drawing to a halt in Leicester Central Station.

I was fascinated by the appearance of the Hall class engines with their warm green livery and orange and black lining, the generous amount of brass-work from the safety-valve cover to the cab sides and splashers, and the magnificent name-plates edged in brass with brass letters, bold against the black background. They were beautiful engines, and it made me want to see more of the Great Western and its larger express locomotive stud.

It was, in fact, my honeymoon in 1957 that first took me deep into Great Western territory and the destination for my new wife and myself was Looe on the Cornish coast. Memories of Paddington and of the Castle class locomotive No 100 A1 *Lloyds* at the head of our train drew me to persuade my bride to walk to the front of the train to see so fine a sight. The engine looked so beautiful that I found it difficult to take my eyes off her. But for me, the true magic of the Cornish branch line was yet to come. At Liskeard we boarded the little two-coach train bound for Looe. The engine was one of the superb 45xx Prairie tank locomotives which I promptly fell in love with (my bride certainly had some competition), and as the journey progressed through wooded valleys filled with dappled sunlight, we were brought to a complete halt at a tiny engine-shed lost deep in the Cornish woods. This was Moorswater, and here we sat while our engine was changed for another of the same class. I could not imagine why the change was necessary, but off we went again, seemingly in the same direction as we had come. However, our destination was eventually reached, only to be found under 2ft of water due to the exceptionally high tides.

Throughout our stay, it was interesting to watch from the window of our room at the hotel as those pretty little tank engines brought in their trains to Looe. More often than not, according to the tide, the engine would come off its train and run forward, its wheels half-submerged in water. A great cascade of sea-water would be thrown up on either side of the line as the engine manoeuvred in the yard ready for its return to Moorswater or Liskeard.

'Dark day at Rugby'
oil painting, 30in × 20in
Memories from my train-spotting days

Before our honeymoon, my wife-to-be had insisted that I take neither paints nor even a sketchbook with me, so that my whole attention might be devoted to her and the enjoyment of our time together. By mid-week however, she realised that I was like a fish out of water and suggested that I purchase a sketchbook without delay. That done, it was soon well used and is still in my studio, complete with the brief sketch that I drew from above the station-yard of the little Prairie tank dashing up the yard, with water cascading in all directions.

So at last I had looked to the West and become entranced with the magnificent delights, both quaint and majestic, of the Great Western Railway. By then, of course, nationalisation had taken place ten years earlier, but of the four main companies, the Great Western had been the least likely to lose either its identity or its pride, so the damage had been negligible.

One of the best thrills of my honeymoon (and there were many that week) had been saved for our return journey. The thoughts of a second glimpse of Brunel's magnificent bridge over the River Taymar at Saltash had certainly been much in mind, but I had not counted for the fact that this time we were to be drawn by an engine of the King class. No 6011 *King James I* sparkled from end to end and if any final nudge were needed to convert a Midland man to the West, then *King James I* did it with consummate ease. These superb locomotives were the largest of all the Great Western 4-6-0s and in 1927 when they were introduced, were the most powerful. Like the Stanier 4-6-2 Coronation class, built some ten years after, they exuded power; it was inherent in every line from the tapered boiler to the massive front bogies and cylinder chests. What a triumph of engineering and artistry combined in these superb locomotives. From that day, the Kings were for me equal to the Coronations of the LMS as the epitome of what an express locomotive should be, not only in terms of performance and power, but as the perfect design from the technical and aesthetic points of view.

Before steam declined, I had many opportunities to watch the giants of the Great Western at work in many locations, but if mention were needed of any in particular, it would perhaps be to single out the coastal run along the Devon stretches of Dawlish, where rough seas can submerge the line, and on to Teignmouth, Torquay, Paignton and Kingswear. The sight of a Castle or King hauling an express on any stretch of that line combined the majesty of steam with unsurpassed natural beauty. Don Breckon's many beautiful paintings of this stretch of our coastline are proof enough of the appeal to the artist's eye of steam by the sea, and Terence Cuneo, too, has shown his predilection for this location, having painted several magnificent oils of this particular stretch.

My first contact with the engines of the Great Western – the Halls – as they appeared on the Leicestershire lines of the Great Central was a portent of things to come later in life; it was in 1978 that I was approached to become the President of the *Witherslack Hall* Locomotive Society, based, as luck would have it, at the Main Line Steam Trust on the lines of the Great Central at Loughborough.

The thought of being associated with the rebuilding of one of these

handsome locomotives appealed to me and I readily agreed. These fast mixed-traffic engines were built from 1928 after an experiment had been made by the rebuilding of the Saint class No 2925 *Saint Martin* with 6ft diameter wheels instead of the original 6ft 8½in. This trial did so well that the new class, named after stately homes throughout the country, eventually numbered as many as 330 locomotives.

Witherslack Hall was bought for £4,500 in 1975 from the scrap-yard at Barry in South Wales. She came to Leicestershire in a rusty, forlorn condition, with far more hope than confidence that she would ever run again or any knowledge as to where the finance for a programme of rebuilding would come from.

The team consisted of no more than eight men headed by Alan Green, their chairman and a railwayman by profession. On my first sight of the engine at Loughborough I was convinced that they would never do it; they had no professional expertise and no money. What they did have was an abundance of enthusiasm and the ability for sheer hard work – months of lying between the main frames scraping off rust is no pleasant way of spending the weekends. Slowly, however, she was dismantled, and equally slowly she rose again in a corner at the far end of the shed. There had been many detractors along the way and many setbacks, so when the great day came for her successful boiler test, the sense of achievement was all the greater because of it.

It would be wrong of me to pretend to anything more than a passive, but sincere, interest over the twelve years of restoration work. As a part of the restoration programme, however, it was suggested that I should paint a portrait of *Witherslack Hall* as she would have appeared within the shed at Old Oak Common. The idea was to produce a fine art print from the painting in order to assist the fund-raising operation. The painting is now in the collection of the National Railway Museum on permanent loan from its owner, Mr Phil Barlow.

On 9 October 1986, a huge crowd, including press and television journalists, stood on the platform at Loughborough Central to witness the renaming ceremony. As the society's President, I had to make a short speech and draw back the curtains over the name-plate. *Witherslack* Hall was in service again. I joined Alan Green, who was to drive that day, on the foot-plate for the first trip up the line, knowing that it was something that Alan had dreamed of and had lived for over the last twelve years, and he described the event to me as the greatest day in his life. Pride filled all our hearts and although my role had only been as an observer over the dozen years of the engine's restoration, it meant a great deal to me also and I reflected on it during our journey. Then it was my turn to sit in the driver's seat to bring the return trip back to Loughborough, and as I opened up the regulator, memories of the Halls that I had seen on the Great Central as a youth came flooding back, and the link, albeit a tenuous one, between these two great railways was re-established.

Castle at Work
oil painting, 30in × 20in
No 7031 'Cromwell's Castle' at speed in the English countryside south of Reading

The story of *Witherslack Hall* is representative of hundreds of other locomotives whose existence has been assured by their purchase and removal from one of the several scrap-yards that destroyed engines at the end of the steam era.

Two graveyards of steam engines existed that were a haunt of mine and where I painted many pictures. The most famous was at Barry Docks, its endless lines of rusting engines making a sad picture for all who had a feeling for the steam locomotive. At its height, there were as many as 750 locomotives awaiting demolition. My pilgrimages to this desolate spot where the chill wind blew its melancholy lament through the sightless hulks of those once magnificent machines, were always with mixed feelings. The engines stood witness to the end of the greatest epoch in our industrial history, and I was always acutely aware that steam transport had begun in South Wales when Richard Trevithick had first run his high-pressure steam locomotive on the Pen-y-darren tram-road at the iron-works of the same name in 1804. So 160 odd years later, I could not help but reflect as I stood among the derelict engines in South Wales that the wheel had turned full circle.

The last consignment of locomotives from British Rail had arrived at Barry in 1967, among them many that had been in service for only a short time. Those handsome standard class 5s, the massive 9s and my favourite BR designs, the Britannias, all with years of working life in them, were discarded as obsolete and abandoned to the ravages of the weather and eventual destruction.

Looking at these images through an artist's eyes brought emotive responses for one so mindful of the glorious past, the proud history of the steam locomotive and all that it meant in our industrial evolution; yet at the same time I responded to the exciting shapes, abstracted by rot or the cutting-torch to rusting remnants. Here was painterly material indeed; on the one hand, textures, colours, harmonies and shapes to please the eye, and on the other, pathos, drama and sadness in the reflections of the end of an era. There was little wonder that one returned again and again, not merely to record but in response to a magnetic compulsion to transmit on canvas my personal feelings on the demise of steam.

At Barry, I painted standard 9s, 5s and 2s, ex-LMS class 5s, and my beloved Jubilees, Great Western panniers, and 45xx tank engines, rusty and derelict, a mighty King, its safety-valve and cover gone, but still hopeful of a reprieve, and those giants from the Southern Railway, the superb *Battle of Britain*, and rebuilt West Country Pacifics that one had admired from a distance in the past, cold and silent in the weeds. Sadly, I probably saw more of the Southern engines at Barry than I had over all the years of my interest in steam.

From Barry it seems right to return to the Midlands and to Kettering in Northamptonshire where so much of my interest in railways was nurtured and where I had watched so much of the workings of the steam age, both in industry and on the lines of the Midland Railway; to look back at Cohen's yard, small by comparison with Barry, but for the artist even more rewarding – it was softer somehow, more atmospheric. Here were mainly North-Eastern

115

S.R. NO. 34073.
"249 SQUADRON"

GWR.
No 5539
Barry Docks
February
1971

'Witherslack Hall'
oil painting, 30in × 20in
No 6990 at Old Oak Common Shed

Rust and weeds at Barry 1971 (pencil sketch)

and Midland engines awaiting their doom, and where inspiration struck with a vengeance at the sight of a half-dismantled carcass of one of Sir William Stanier's marvellous class 5s – 'Mickeys' we called them as children. Eventually, a large canvas was produced of that emotive vision, an anonymous, numberless wreck, but of all the sights I had witnessed in the scrap-yards of the Sixties, this skeletonic image symbolised everything there was to say about the end of the steam locomotive.

'A Carcass at Kettering' became part of the set of canvases describing the history of the British steam locomotive. When it finally went on show in London, more than one person came to me to talk about it with tears in their eyes, and it continues to have this evocative effect. That is, perhaps, the greatest compliment that could be paid to an artist, and confirmation enough that hand and eye, paint and emotion, inspiration and experience, had surely come together in the effort to communicate.

Today one hears much about nostalgia for things past and regret at the loss of the old ways of life, progress and modernisation eliminating much of character in favour of the standard and the purely utilitarian. In looking back as a painter of the railway scene, I can only rejoice that I have been fortunate enough to live through those last decades of the steam age, and trust that what is transmitted through the brush is a true reflection of how it was, not over-sentimentalised or glamorised, but an honest attempt to make a portrayal on canvas from the heart.

If there is any consolation for the artist in his struggle to overcome the myriad of complexities encountered in the business of communicating through paint, it is the knowledge that his efforts have been done with sincerity. Then at least he is not hiding from his own conscience when his work is on public display.

During my forty years of picture-making, I have been attracted to almost every type of subject matter that is possible to paint, but I have found that steam locomotives and their attendant backgrounds are the most difficult subjects to portray. In this respect, it would seem that I and my fellow artists in the field take a strange delight in our painstaking work.

Whatever the difficulties, however, I am sure that I will continue to paint pictures of the steam age, not only for my own pleasure or for the pleasure of those who knew it, but for the sake of future generations, so that they, too, may savour the spirit of a great epoch as seen through the eyes of those who have been blessed with a passion for paint and the love of steam.

(page 118) 'The King awaits a reprieve'
oil painting, 16in × 12in

(page 119) 'A Carcass at Kettering'
oil painting, 60in × 50in
From the final triptych of paintings in The History of the British Steam Locomotive Collection